Advance Praise ʃ
CALM BREATH, CALM MIND

"This work is a fascinating introduction to the Bönpo tradition of secret breathing yoga, revealing how to integrate breath in order to improve meditation, as well as to restore physical health through specific yogic techniques. The teachings are clear and easy to apply both in daily life and in retreat."

—Jean-Luc Achard, researcher at the Centre National de la Recherche Scientifique and author of *The Six Lamps*

"I welcome this second edition of Geshe YongDong's *Calm Breath, Calm Mind*, which shares a range of practices with breath at its center. His simple and direct style of teachings comes through in the book. The practices he presents here range from simple breathings to breathings with visualizations, sounds, and the movements of *tsa lung trul khor*, the five magical movements. The simple instructions enable the reader to perform them and discover the healing potential in their lives."

—Alejandro Chaoul, author of *Tibetan Yoga* and *Tibetan Yoga for Health & Well-Being*

"Grown up in the ancient Bön tradition in Tibet and living in Canada, Geshe YongDong is able to express the tradition's deep practices in accessible language with a poetic undertone. Through simple exercises, taking breath and energy as the overriding theme, he leads us to experience a deep sense of inner peace and well-being. If you are new to meditation, here is an excellent guide to develop an authentic and effective practice. If you are an experienced practitioner, this book will reconnect you to an attitude of openness and playfulness in your practice."

—Florens van Canstein, meditation teacher and translator in the Bön tradition and author of *Travelling with the Master*

དབུགས

CALM BREATH, CALM MIND

A Guide to the Healing Power of Breath

Geshe YongDong Losar

TRANSCRIBED AND EDITED BY
Bernadette Wyton

FOREWORD BY
Geshe Tenzin Wangyal Rinpoche

Wisdom

Wisdom Publications
199 Elm Street
Somerville, MA 02144 USA
wisdomexperience.org

First edition self-published in 2017.

Library of Congress Cataloging-in-Publication Data
Names: Losar, Geshe YongDong, 1969– author. | Wyton, Bernadette, editor. |
    Wangyal, Tenzin, writer of introduction.
Title: Calm breath, calm mind: a guide to the healing power of breath /
    Geshe YongDong Losar; transcribed and edited by Bernadette Wyton;
    foreword by Geshe Tenzin Wangyal Rinpoche.
Description: Second edition. | Somerville: Wisdom Publications, 2022.
Identifiers: LCCN 2021060232 (print) | LCCN 2021060233 (ebook) |
    ISBN 9781614297802 (paperback) | ISBN 9781614298014 (ebook)
Subjects: LCSH: Ānāpānasmṛti. | Respiration—Religious aspects—Buddhism.
Classification: LCC BQ5630.A6 L67 2022 (print) | LCC BQ5630.A6 (ebook) |
    DDC 294.3/443—dc23/eng/20220202
LC record available at https://lccn.loc.gov/2021060232
LC ebook record available at https://lccn.loc.gov/2021060233

ISBN 978-1-61429-780-2   ebook ISBN 978-1-61429-801-4

26 25 24 23 22   5 4 3 2 1

Cover design by Phil Pascuzzo. Interior design by Gopa & Ted2, Inc.
All Tibetan calligraphy is by Geshe YongDong Losar, including the Uchen character
for "Breath" on page ii. The line drawings of Geshela are © Gillian Brooks.
The diagram of energy channels and chakras is © Lhari Kalsang Nyima.
The photograph of Geshela is © Gordon Ross.

Printed on acid-free paper that meets the guidelines for permanence and durability of
the Production Guidelines for Book Longevity of the Council on Library Resources.

Printed in the United States of America.

MIX
Paper from
responsible sources
FSC® C005010

Please visit fscus.org.

To my Amala, Norma Forrest

Contents

Foreword   ix

Preface to the Second Edition   xi

Introduction: Trust the Guide, Commit to the Path   1

PART I. THE ESSENCE OF BREATH

1. Breath of Life   7

2. The Three Dimensions of *Lung* Energy   13

3. The Five *Lung* Energies   23

4. Middle and Lower Breath Exercises   31

PART II. THE HEALING POWER OF BREATH

5. The Meaning of Healing   39

6. Riding the Breath   51

7. The Healing Practice of Tonglen   55

PART III. BREATH AND MEDITATION

8. Meditation and the Mind   65

9. How to Meditate   71

10. Calm-Abiding Meditation   79

11. Insight Meditation   85

12. It Makes a Difference   93

Part IV. Breath and Visualization

13. Seeing in a Different Way   103

14. The Nine-Breath Purification Practice   107

Part V. Breath and Movement

15. The Body–Mind Connection   117

16. The Five Magic Movements   123

Part VI. Breath and Sound

17. Mantra: The Voice of Meditation   139

18. Seed Syllables   147

19. Connecting to Five Warrior Qualities   153

20. The Five Warrior Seed Syllable Practice   159

Conclusion   165

Appendix 1. The Tibetan Bön Tradition   167

Appendix 2. Bön Cosmology   175

Notes   181

About the Author   183

Foreword

IT IS WONDERFUL to see this very helpful book by Geshe YongDong manifest. It offers a wide variety of simple, direct, profound exercises of the breath (Skt: *prana*, Tib: *lung*), each of which has the power to enhance well-being on many different levels of body, energy, and mind.

The pages to come feature exercises specifically intended for calming and stabilizing the mind, others for clearing the body's subtle channels and energy centers of blockages and disturbances, and still others for cultivating open awareness. The exercises are presented in a way that nearly anyone can understand and perform. At the same time, Geshe YongDong goes into depth and detail regarding the ancient Tibetan Bön Buddhist traditions. Throughout, he lends many insights gained from his years of practice and of teaching Western students, as well as the knowledge he has drawn from the ancient, authentic texts that are at the source of these practices.

Geshe YongDong's esteemed root lamas are His Holiness Lungtok Tenpai Nyima, the Thirty-Third Menri Trizin; His Eminence Yongdzin Tenzin Namdak Rinpoche; and the Venerable Gyaltshab Tenzin Wangyal Rinpoche. In 1992, he received his *geshe* degree, the equivalent to a Western PhD in theology, from Nangzhig Bönpo Monastery in Tibet. After further in-depth study at Sera Monastic University and Menri Monastery in India, and then teaching in France, he traveled to Canada in 1999 and has lived and taught there since. In 2003, he established Sherab Chamma Ling, a Tibetan Bön Buddhist center in Courtenay, British Columbia.

I have known Geshe YongDong for many long years and consider him a good friend. Like him, I have a longtime interest in practices of the breath. Over and over I have personally witnessed, both in myself and in my students, the breath's clear potential to heal and deeply transform lives. I truly believe that in the future such practices will play an important role as a medicine for preventing and treating physical, emotional, and mental maladies.

I am glad that Geshe YongDong is making these practices widely available, and I'm sure that by doing so, he is bringing benefit to countless lives.

Geshe Tenzin Wangyal Rinpoche

Preface to the Second Edition

I have a special gift for you.
It's the most precious thing I have to offer
and is the only thing I carried with me out of Tibet.
I am passing it on to you now, knowing that it could help you
as much as it has helped me.

THE TEACHINGS IN THIS BOOK provide clear instructions for using the breath to balance and heal body and mind. They were given to me by spiritual masters, who received them from their teachers in the long chain of giving and receiving that has created the Tibetan Bon lineage. They point to the indestructible source of meaning and value, of joy and contentment, and of physical and mental well-being.

I have been sharing this knowledge over many years through the spoken word in workshops and retreats. In 2017, the first edition of *Calm Breath, Calm Mind* was self-published as the first written collection of my teachings and my first book written in English; something I had wanted to do ever since arriving in Canada. It has served well as a concise handbook on how to use breath and vital energy to restore and maintain balance and healing.

In preparing to go to print again, I was given the opportunity to revise the book and publish a second edition with Wisdom Publications. The result is a better organized guide that provides a deeper look into breath in relation to healing, meditation, visualization, and movement along with a completely new section on breath and sound.

My first teachings on the healing power of breath were given in

Port Alberni, British Columbia, Canada, in 2008 and 2011. My writing assistant, Bernadette Wyton, produced a word-for-word transcript of the 2011 session that was used as a starting point for collaborative work that would unfold over the next six years, resulting in the first edition of this book.

The process of "re-vision" has been a wonderful opportunity to step back, take a fresh look, and return to writing with greatly enhanced tools. My ability to speak and read English has improved, my audience has expanded, my teaching and writing sessions have been facilitated by online video meetings, and the collaboration necessary for transcribing has become a seamless and richly rewarding effort.

Another first for me, and something I particularly enjoyed, was creating the poetry for the beginning of each chapter in this book. Again, this was my first attempt at expressing myself in this way in English. When I sat down to try my hand at the task, the first six poems flowed out of me in about ten minutes. All of the poems have been transcribed with great care to provide my heartfelt wonder and connection to the healing power of breath. I still love reading them and the way they impart the beauty and essence of the message while providing a pause before entering the chapter.

I remember my auntie, who always encouraged my studies, used to say, "The Dharma, what you are learning, is something you can use forever. It is yours, and no one can ever steal it from you." As a young teenager, I didn't really understand what she meant.

But she was right. In a matter of years, in order to escape the oppression in Tibet, I lost everything I had except for the spiritual training that had become a part of me. The riches of the Dharma accompanied me to where I am now in Canada and will continue to do so beyond this life. I offer many of those riches to you now, as a gift, with my blessing and wish for your temporal and ultimate benefit.

Come, unwrap the Dharma.

ACKNOWLEDGMENTS

There are many devoted students, friends, and colleagues who have helped to make this book possible. I extend my deepest appreciation to them for their support and guidance.

Special thanks go to the following:

My longtime friend Geshe Kalsang Gyatso, for his help clarifying the lineage and practice of the five *tsa lung* movements.

Dr. Tom Diamond, for reviewing drafts and suggesting improvements.

Gillian Brooks, for providing the exercise illustrations.

Lhari Kalsang Nyima, for providing the diagram of energy channels and chakras.

Gordon Ross, for his portrait photography and his help with my calligraphy reproductions.

Bernadette Wyton, my longtime friend and dedicated student who has done an amazing job capturing in writing what I've meant through the spoken word, in English, which is my second language. She has worked with me over many years, transcribing my teachings in a way that is as clear, simple, and inspiring as possible while remaining true to the lineage. Without her effort, writing this book would not have been possible.

And, lastly, Amala, Norma Forrest, my late, beloved, spiritual, adopted mother who took me under her wing while I was still a refugee trying to settle within a new land, language, and culture. Her guidance, caring, wisdom, and protection helped shape who I am now as a person, as a Canadian citizen, and as a Tibetan Bön teacher in the West. I will always cherish the memory of her constant encouragement and her whole-hearted dedication to me and to the Tibetan Bön lineage. She helped me in so many ways, including the many hours by my side reviewing this book.

Geshe YongDong
Courtenay, British Columbia

Introduction: Trust the Guide, Commit to the Path

If you are lost, breath will find you.
If you are stressed, it will relieve you.
If you are wandering, it will bring you home.
If you are confused, it will blow away the clouds.

INSTRUCTOR AND GUIDE

CALM BREATH, CALM MIND is a guide to the healing power of breath, one that is suitable for both beginners and experienced practitioners. It is full of information and directions for many different ways of using the breath to restore and maintain physical and mental well-being. Connecting to just one of them could change your life.

Although the subtitle of this book is "A Guide to the Healing Power of Breath," in truth, the healer *and* the guide are breath itself. In this sense, the book is like an instructor who introduces you to the guide—to breath. As you come to understand the instructor and the subject of breath, they unify and come to life, off the page, through your own experience of breath connecting body and mind, self and other, inner and outer.

This book is intended as a resource you can carry with you through your life, not something to read once and leave behind. This is because of three reasons: First, you can't remember or experience everything at once. Second, you may resonate with some methods at one time but with others at another time as you and the circumstances around you change. And third, the effectiveness of this guide and the healing power of breath itself depends on your commitment, training, and effort over time. It can only provide guidance if you are moving on a spiritual path, not sitting back, passively waiting for results.

The information provided in *Calm Breath, Calm Mind* is foundational. As such, if you come to know it well, it will help bring clarity and guidance to anything else you choose to study.

Trust the guide; commit to the path.

SOURCE AND PURPOSE

I was born into the mysterious and wonderful world of Bön, the original, indigenous, spiritual tradition of Tibet. The history of Bön goes back many, many thousands of years to the enlightenment of the buddha Tönpa Shenrab[1] and the first teachings he gave to help a primitive people who, at the time, had little readiness or capacity to understand his wisdom. Over the millennia, the essence of the Buddha's knowledge and teachings found a home in what is now known as Yungdrung Bön.[2]

Yung means "no beginning" or "birthless." *Drung* means "no end" or "deathless." Yungdrung Bön illuminates the path to our true nature that is beyond birth and death, beyond the suffering of our dualistic, egocentric state of mind. It teaches how to wake up, just as Tönpa Shenrab did, to who we truly are.

In the English language, those who realize their true nature are called "awakened." In Sanskrit, they are called *buddha*. In Tibetan they are called *sang gye*: *sang* means "awakened" and *gye* means "fully developed" or "increasing." *Sang gye* refers to awakening from the sleep of delusion, affliction, and ignorance into the expanding fullness of wisdom-awareness. This awakening is the ultimate goal of all of the teachings and methods shared by all of the buddhas, or *sang gyes*, and it is the ultimate purpose of the teachings I share with you in this book.

POWER AND POTENTIAL

Energy is the basis of everything. When we are challenged physically and/or mentally, many of us first seek relief through medication, exercise, or special food while completely ignoring the underlying energetic imbalance. No matter what we eat or how much we exercise, we will not feel well again until that balance is restored.

If you feel chronically disconnected from your true nature, from who you are, your soul or spirit (in Tibetan, *la*)³ may wander and become lost. This kind of disconnect is at the root of the anxiety and depression that is epidemic in the world today.

The first step in reconnecting to yourself is connecting to your breath, which will restore balance. This can clear the mind, filling it with light, and energize the body, filling it with fresh air.

If you are lost, breath will find you; if you are stressed, it will relieve you; if you are wandering, it will bring you home; if you are confused, it will blow away the clouds of thoughts and emotions.

Mindfulness of breathing is an effective tool for training and focusing the mind. Once you are familiar with it, you can direct your mind to any task or intention. Everything you feel, think, and do will be more balanced and connected.

In the coming chapters I will describe a number of ways to use the breath within the disciplines of meditation, visualization, mantra recitation, and movement. All of these methods serve to settle your body and mind in their natural state, which is beyond whatever is holding you back—beyond your ego, your hopes and fears, your past and future. With proper training, they reduce negative emotions and automatically open the gates of wisdom, understanding, compassion, and loving kindness.

GETTING THERE

So, what is your ultimate purpose or goal? What is your destination in life?

Most people just want to break the bonds of whatever is keeping them from being fulfilled, happy, and free of suffering. But how do you get there?

You must discover a way that is proven to be effective, something you can place your trust in to get you to your destination. Most of us know how to turn outward for help and safety, and many may recognize the terms for taking outer refuge in the enlightened teachers (*lama, buddha*), the authentic teachings (*dharma*), and the community of awakening travelers (*sangha*). However, in these pages is an introduction to the *innermost* form of refuge.

In the Bön view, the vehicle that can carry you to the ultimate goal is the vital energy of your own breath (*lung*), and the path is the energetic highways or channels (*tsa*) within your body. And it is the light of awareness within your own sacred mind (*tigle*) that is in the driver's seat. These three are objects of the deepest form of refuge. They can keep you safe and free of suffering. Indeed, they can save your life.

As you engage in the work described here, you will come to view and value your own body, mind, and energy as sacred. You will come to know that you don't have to look somewhere else for healing and protection: you have the ability, potential, and resources within to enter the fullness of who you are.

PART I

The Essence of Breath

1: Breath of Life

When I fully connect to the breath, I am the breath.
Breath is me.
We embrace each other and become one.

THE TIBETAN WORD *LUNG*

OVER MILLENNIA, many Eastern traditions have developed practices that use the powerful healing energy of breath to treat physical, emotional, and mental problems. In Chinese, this energy is called *chi*, in Indian Sanskrit it is called *prana*, and in Tibetan it is called *lung*.

For clarity, the Tibetan word *lung* will remain italicized throughout this book. It is pronounced "loong" and is not to be confused with the English word for the physical organ of breathing, the lung.

Lung is a difficult word to translate into English. Terms such as "breath," "wind," "air," "energy," and "life force" are used interchangeably for *lung*, but none of them contain its full meaning.

To explain, consider that white horses are horses, but horses are not necessarily white. They can also be black, brown, pinto, and palomino. In the same way, breath is *lung*, but *lung* is not necessarily breath.

One way to understand *lung* is to think of it as the essence of breath. *Lung* and breath are not separate, which is why the words are often used for each other.

Another way to understand *lung* is to think of it as the movement of energy. In the Tibetan language, *lung* literally means "wind" or "air." Wind is always moving and has a natural energy to blow away and purify. For example, it dilutes and blows away smoke, smells, and other forms of air pollution. It also purifies, like a fresh breeze passing through old clothes hung out on a line.

In addition to the outer form of *lung*—wind energy—there is the inner form, which is known as "inner air." This refers to the movement of energy within our body. Inner air has the energy to purify inner pollution, which is experienced as physical, mental, and emotional disturbances.

Lung is life-giving energy and a lack of it results in a lack of energy for body and mind. For example, when someone dies, their heart is still there but it has no *lung* energy. It is *lung* that drives our beating heart, not the heart itself.

As we become aware of breath and *lung* through practice, we become aware of everything around us, making it possible to experience our true nature.

INDIVIDUAL AND UNIVERSAL BREATH

There are two types of breath: individual and universal.

From the day we are born until we die, every breath we take is individual breath. Your breath is individual breath, and my breath is individual breath.

According to the creation story from the Bön tantric tradition, the great god Trigyal Khugpa[4] created the universe by blowing his breath out into the emptiness of space, imparting life to the entire universe. When you inhale, this general breath becomes your individual breath. As soon as you exhale, that breath is no longer your own. It merges back into universal breath.

We are all connected to each other through individual and universal breath. The atoms and molecules we breathe have been recycled again and again through many plants and beings over many centuries. We are on the same earth breathing the same air that came and went from the lungs of Buddha, Jesus, and Mahatma Gandhi. This fact alone is a great focus for meditation.

Please remember how precious the breath of life is for every living thing. When you look at someone, try to remember that they, like you, are alive because they are breathing. When you see a flower, a tree, a river, or even the ocean, be aware that they also have life because they are breathing. This beautiful planet is a living, breathing miracle.

IT'S ALL IN THE BALANCE

Whether in the collective life of the world or in an individual's life, it is very important that *lung* energy be balanced. Collective imbalances can lead to natural disasters, and individual imbalances can lead to physical and emotional turmoil.

When *lung* is imbalanced, your energy is negative. This is known as *samsaric lung*. As it moves within you, it creates disturbances, blockages, and obstacles for your body, mind, and spirit. This may result in the suffering of physical and mental illnesses. It can also lead to emotional struggles expressed as confusion, anger, depression, attachment, and agitation.

For example, anger arises as an expression of imbalanced inner *lung* energy. Tibetans call an angry person *lung ling*, which literally means "arise *lung*"—the arising of inner wind or air. As anger rises, *lung* also pushes blood into the upper body. Mental function becomes abnormal, clarity decreases, and perceptions of what another says and does become distorted by the pollution of one's own mind.

When *lung* energy is balanced, it is less likely that anger will surface. Challenging speech and actions do not easily disturb someone whose inner space of *lung* is open and balanced.

When *lung* is balanced, it is positive, and your energy is positive. This is known as *nirvanic lung*. It is uplifting, like the wind whisking a piece of paper off the ground. As it moves within you, it supports your inner organs and your general health. It helps your mind to be clear and positive, which strengthens the qualities of loving-kindness and openness. The experience of body and mind functioning in harmony is the experience of *nirvanic lung*.

RESPIRATION

Have you ever really thought about how important breath is to you or how it affects your body and mind?

Take a moment right now to relax and do an easy breathing exercise:

- Sit or stand comfortably with your hands at your sides.
- Inhale slowly and deeply through your nose, keeping your mouth closed.
- Hold the breath for few seconds.
- Exhale by slowly blowing the breath out between your lips.
- Stop reading now. Practice for five minutes and see what happens.

When you are finished, try to notice any effect the exercise has had on your mind, body, or energy. You will probably find that your mind is quieter with fewer thoughts, that your body is calm and more relaxed, that your heart rate is lower, and that you are enjoying various pleasant sensations.

Now, consider what is happening when you inhale and exhale:

- When you breathe in, your diaphragm moves down, making more space for your lungs as they fill with air.
- The air travels deep into your lungs, reaching the alveoli, the tiny air sacs within the lungs where oxygen is transferred from the air into the bloodstream, while carbon dioxide is transferred from the bloodstream into the air.
- As you exhale, your diaphragm relaxes and helps push the carbon dioxide and stale air out of your lungs.

At this physical level, we can see how important the breath is for survival. It carries and supports us from the first breath we draw at birth to the last breath we release at death. But breath has far more meaning than most people ever think about.

The true nature of breath at the more subtle, underlying energetic level requires a deeper understanding. For thousands of years, Tibetans have studied this moving energy and have developed breathing techniques to help generate calmness, strength, and healing for the body and clarity for the mind. By using our breath mindfully, we can do amazing things to improve our ordinary lives.

BREATHING UNDERWATER

Breathing mindfully can be integrated into anything we are doing. Here is an example of just how effective calming the breath can be:

A few years ago, while on a teaching trip to Central America, I took a few scuba diving lessons. I love swimming and all water sports, and this was the first time for me to try swimming underwater with all the scuba equipment.

I enjoyed the lessons and was fully focused on them, but no matter how hard I tried to go under the water, I floated up to the top. The instructor, whose English was not that good either, tried to help and gave his best advice, but it was no good; it seemed like my body was just not meant to go down.

I went with the instructor and the other, more experienced, scuba students to a good diving location where we could even see sharks. We took our scuba-certification test there, and everyone got their certification except me. I tried so hard and was a little embarrassed, but it was no use. I could not force my body down; my head kept pointing up and so I failed.

Later, when I thought about what I was doing wrong, I realized I was not relaxed in my body or my breath. I had been too tense and nervous trying to follow the instructor's directions. Each time I tried and failed, I became more tense, and my breathing became more shallow.

Normally, I am a deep breather and am very relaxed. I have since gone underwater many times at the swimming pool in my town and now find it easy to control my body with my breathing. I can even sit on the bottom of the pool for several minutes. My swimming friends tell me I am like a fish because I can stay under the water for such a long time.

So, remember, breathing is a very powerful, calming tool. When your breathing is relaxed, your body is relaxed as well as your mind. It all works together.

The dramatic change that just a few breaths can make points to the potential of regular breathing practice. Consistent practice is key to healing, even of disorders related to stress, anxiety, addiction, or other chronic disturbances. However, it takes time, experience, and commitment for the full benefit of breathing exercises to emerge.

2: The Three Dimensions of *Lung* Energy

My body is like a lotus flower.
My breath is like a pond to nurture my body.
My mind is like a fish enjoying them both.
I am fullness when I recognize it.

Lung FLOWS in three different dimensions, or levels:

1. gross or outer *lung*, which is easily perceived by our senses;
2. subtle or inner *lung*, which moves through the hidden channels of our bodies;
3. subtle-inherent or secret *lung*, which is primordial, unchanging, and beyond normal perception.

GROSS *LUNG*

The movement of *lung* that can be seen, heard, and felt is called *lung ragpa* in Tibetan, which literally means "gross *lung* energy." For example, when you breathe in and out, or blow breath on your hand, you can feel and hear the breath. *Lung* is obvious at this physical, outer level of air energy.

Gross *lung* is also the movement of energy related to the five organs (heart, lungs, liver, kidney, spleen), the five senses (eye, nose, ear, tongue, body), and the five limbs (head, right arm, left arm, right leg, left leg). How does this energy develop? Is there an energetic process related to physical development?

The answer is yes. Starting at conception, through incredibly intricate processes of growth and transformation, these energy systems evolve, each in their own ascending order as described below. They continue to grow and develop until adulthood and are then constantly renewed until death.

In the mother's womb, the first *lung* energy of the five organs to develop is that of the heart organ followed by the lungs, liver, kidneys, and spleen. All this growing activity is generated and supported by gross *lung* energy.

At the same time, the senses and limbs are also developing. The first *lung* energy of the five senses to develop is that of the eye, followed by the nose, tongue, ear, and body or flesh.

The first *lung* energy of the five limbs to develop is that of the head, followed by the right leg, right arm, left leg, and left arm.

At death, these energetic systems collapse, simultaneously, in the reverse order. For example, the spleen's *lung* energy dissolves back into kidney energy that in turn dissolves back into liver energy, then lung energy, and finally heart energy. When the heart dies, gross *lung* energy is completed or finished. Gross *lung* then dissolves into subtle *lung*, and when subtle *lung* is complete, it dissolves into subtle-inherent *lung*.

The dissolving *lung* energy process is understood in the Tibetan tradition as two stages of death, outer and inner. When the dissolution of energy from the five organs, five senses, and five limbs is complete, outer death has occurred. The inner stage of death is a process that takes place at the subtle *lung* energy level.

SUBTLE *LUNG*

Subtle *lung*, known as *lung trawa*, supports the health and function of the entire body and is beyond what is normally visible for the ordinary mind. It flows through unseen channels within the body called *tsa*. Along these pathways are energy hubs known as chakras, or *khorlos* (literally "wheels"), which serve as collection and distribution centers. In this system within the body there are three main *lung* or energy channels and five main *lung* or energy chakras.

From the top of our head to the bottom of our feet, there are 72,000 subtle *lung* energy systems. They can be enriched by many different healing and health-promoting methods, such as acupuncture, yoga, breathing exercises, and other forms of meditation.

THREE MAIN CHANNELS

central, blue channel	*tsa uma*
right, white channel	*tsa kyangma*
left, red channel	*tsa roma*

FIVE MAIN CHAKRAS

crown chakra	*chiwo dechen khorlo*	wheel of great bliss at the crown
throat chakra	*drinpa longchod khorlo*	wheel of enjoyment at the throat
heart chakra	*nyinka bonid khorlo*	wheel of emptiness at the heart
navel chakra	*tewa trulwey khorlo*	wheel of manifestation at the navel
secret place chakra	*sangney dechong khorlo*	wheel of generating bliss at the secret place

All movement of *lung* energy in the body originates from within the three main channels. The central channel is the essence of an individual. It runs through the middle of the torso, along the inside of the spine. It is visualized as a straight, glowing, blue column running from the top of the head to the "secret place" at the base of the torso, where the reproductive organs reside. The top of the channel at the crown is wider than the bottom. Tibetans often liken it to a poppy flower, with the wider opening at the crown of the head and the long stem running down to the base of the body.

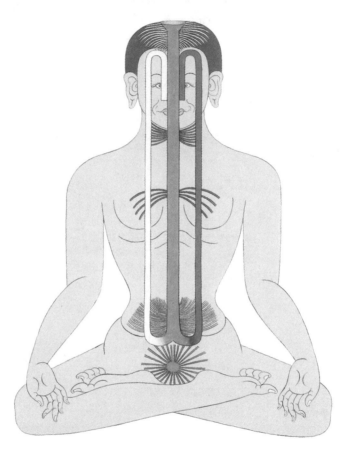

The channel to the right of the central one (that is, the person's right; from the perspective of someone looking at this person, the channel would be to their left) is visualized as white, signifying bone. This channel is viewed as the essence of life inherited from the father.

The channel to the left of the central channel is seen as red, signifying blood. This is the essence of life inherited from the mother. The two side channels are thinner than the central one and run parallel to it until entering the skull. There they flow along the inside of the skull and follow its curve up over the brain until finally dropping down behind the eyes and exiting through the nostrils.

SUBTLE-INHERENT *LUNG*

Subtle-inherent *lung* is known as *lhankye kyi lung*, which literally means "inherent energy." It is also called *nyug me lung*, which means "primordial energy." It manifests out of the emptiness of infinite space, which is the base or foundation of the universe and is called the *künzhi* (*kün* means "all" and *zhi* means "base").

This *lung* supports primordial awareness and enlightenment. It also supports what is known as the base consciousness, or the *künzhi namshe* (*namshe* means "consciousness"), from which all other forms of consciousness arise.[5]

Subtle-inherent *lung* is changeless, constant, has always been there, and is present in the same way for all living beings. It is indescribable, but it can be experienced once a practitioner reaches beyond the ordinary thinking mind.

When the body dies, gross *lung* dissolves into subtle *lung*, which then dissolves back into subtle-inherent *lung*. This subtle-inherent *lung* is the vehicle that carries the consciousness from one lifetime into the next. Like consciousness itself, subtle-inherent *lung* is never born and never dies.

Another way of understanding subtle-inherent *lung* is to consider its movement at two levels—ultimate and relative. At the ultimate level, it is the base of everything, including gross and subtle *lung*. At the relative level, it carries our life, second by second, day by day, until we die.

Each breath we take is the movement of relative subtle-inherent *lung*. In twenty-four hours, there are 21,600 movements of subtle-inherent *lung* in the 21,600 breath movements (inhalations and exhalations) that we take during that period.

From those movements of energy, the countless feelings and activities of our lives manifest. Subtle-inherent *lung* is the root of joy and depression, good and bad choices, right and wrong activities, feelings of contentment or regret, falling asleep and waking up, birth and death.

Subtle-inherent *lung* is also the root of the constant stream of our thoughts and emotions. Ancient Tibetan texts say that in one day, 84,000 thoughts and emotions will arise. There are 86,400 seconds in a day, so almost every second subtle-inherent *lung* is moving in this way.

We become aware of the primordial *lung* energy through meditation and, in doing so, connect with our own primordial awareness, wisdom, and compassion. That connection leads to the purification of obstacles and, eventually, to enlightenment.

LUNG AT CONCEPTION, BIRTH, AND DEATH

It is very important to know about the nature of one's own body, its physical development, and the underlying flow of subtle energy that supports it.

In the West, it seems to me that conception is generally understood as the union of sperm and egg without much consideration given to how *lung* energy and consciousness support the baby's formation. Tibetans believe that consciousness begins at conception, beyond the physical form of the fertilized egg. It is seen as foundational to the development of the brain, organs, senses, and limbs, along with the baby's energetic, emotional, and mental growth. The appearance of form is inseparable from the development of *lung* energy.

At the physical level, gross *lung* also begins with the union of sperm and egg. As soon as the egg is fertilized, five main *lung* energies arise to support the baby's five main organs, five senses, five limbs, five aggregates (form, feeling, perception, mental formation, consciousness), and five elements (space, wind, fire, water, earth). Those five lung energies are called *tsa wai lung nga*: *tsa wai* means "root," *lung* means "energy," and *nga* means "five." Gross *lung* is the vehicle by which these systems grow and function.

As we've discussed, the foundation of gross *lung* is subtle *lung* and the foundation of subtle *lung* is subtle-inherent *lung*. During the birth process, these forms of energy arise one out of the other, just as at death they fall back and dissolve one into the other.

Subtle *lung* has its own ascending and descending process at birth and death. It is expressed in three stages of *lung* energy called the energy of black near-attainment, the energy of red increase, and the energy of white appearance.

The subtle energy of black near-attainment appears from primordial *lung* at the first moment of conception, when the sperm and egg unite. It is a subconscious state of awareness, pulsing under the radar screen of consciousness. It is like looking out into space on a very dark night and seeing nothing, yet still knowing and feeling the energy of the universe.

After conception, a movement of energy arises that has the appearance of red increase. This is comparable to staring into a sun-filled sky and then shutting your eyes. Everything looks red.

Then there is the energy of white appearance, which is similar to staring into moonlight and then shutting your eyes. Everything is white.

Remember that your body is created from the body of your mother and father. The energy of red increase in your body is inherited from your mother. The essence of your blood comes from your mother, and because blood is red, this energy is called "red" increase. It pulses through your left, red energy channel.

The energy of white appearance in your body is inherited from your father. The essence of your bone comes from your father, and because bone is white, this energy is called "white" appearance. It pulses through your right, white energy channel.

The energy of black near-attainment is your own unique energy that comes from the unified essence of the father and the mother. It pulses in the core of your being through the central, blue energy channel. This color is such a dark blue that it is called "black" near-attainment.

The descriptions given above are very basic. Some explanations of channel visualization switch the sides of the red and white channels based on gender, but this is an unnecessary complication at this point. The main thing to understand is that you are both male and female. The expression of this is extremely complicated and varies from one individual to the next.

From ancient times, Tibetans have viewed the expression of gender within five classes:

- male (*pho*)
- female (*mo*)
- transgender (*manang*, used to mean those with no gender or sexual organs and those with both male and female sexual organs, etc.)
- feminine (*mosham*, refers to those who have pronounced features, attitudes, and behaviors considered to be feminine)
- and very feminine (*shindu mo*, refers to those with exaggerated characteristics considered to be feminine).

Energy is also viewed on a gender scale, from rough, strong, male energy through increasingly more feminine expressions. Tibetans even view the alphabet with this kind of gender scale, running from the rough, strong sounds of what are considered male letters through the increasingly softer and gentler sounds of female letter categories.

ENERGY LOSS THROUGH THE NINE DOORS

In the Tibetan view, the human body has nine openings, or doors, called *pukha go gu*. They are the mouth, left nostril, right nostril, left ear, right ear, left eye, right eye, anus, and external urinary orifice. They act as doorways of purification and release, excreting various products of metabolism such as tears, ear wax, feces, and urine. They are also portals of energy exchange and potential energy loss.

Every day we lose large quantities of *lung* energy through these doors. It's easy to understand how this might happen through the high-energy systems of elimination, but energy is also lost at a much subtler level through all of the doors.

For example, we "see" form through the doorway of our eyes, but the mind interprets and attaches to form as an object. Mind and energy can wander out and be lost to objects through the door of the eyes. In the same way, mind and energy can be lost into an object of touch or an object of any of the other doors.

Understanding the nature of energy loss through the nine doors is especially important at death. At this time, as the energy systems of the body dissolve one after another into the central channel and finally into the heart, the consciousness or soul of an individual must leave.

It is most desirable that this essence be ejected from the crown chakra, not lost, misdirected, or dribbled away through any of the doors of the body. Closing the nine doors with awareness ensures that ejection through the crown is the path of least resistance.

Phowa practice is a method for transferring the consciousness up through the central energy channel and out through the top of the head. Practicing phowa during our lifetime should make this easier to accomplish during the dying process. It is necessary to receive the instruction and transmission for this profound practice from a qualified master.

Many buddhas and masters died in the classic lion posture, where one lies on the right side with the right hand under the head and the left hand resting on the left hip. In this posture, the five fingers of the right hand holding the head symbolize closing the upper sense doors located in the head. The fingers of the left hand symbolize closing the bottom doors, called *ogo* in Tibetan.

In the Hindu tradition, closing the doors of the five senses with the hand is a symbol of meditation and focusing inwards. Many are familiar with the classic "see no evil, hear no evil, speak no evil" monkey images, each covering a different sense-door with their hands. They remind us not to wander and lose *lung* energy through our senses of sight, smell, taste, hearing, and touch.

3. The Five *Lung* Energies

My body is the sacred land.
My channel is the sacred path.
Lung-breath is the medicine for both.
Mind-awareness is the essential guide for all of them.

I AM VERY EXCITED to share with you some of what I have learned from my culture about our basic energetic makeup. This is a complicated topic, but I will briefly summarize it here so that even if you were unfamiliar with the concepts, you can begin to experience some of the well-being that comes from visualizing and using the *lung* energies in the following breathing exercises.

Movement of the five main *lung* energies along energy channels within the body maintains the *lung* energies of the five organs, five limbs, five senses, and so on. These main *lungs* are considered the root, or source, of all the other 72,000 *lungs* within our body. They are named according to the main character of their movement or activity, which is likened to air or wind.

upward moving wind	*gyen gyul lung*
life-force wind	*sok dzin kyi lung*
fire-like wind	*menyam kyi lung*
pervasive wind	*khaypjé kyi lung*
downward clearing wind	*thursel kyi lung*

To get a sense of the nature of these energies, consider the process of digestion. Chewing food involves the action of the upward moving wind energy. Swallowing and the movement of food into the stomach is the action or work of the downward clearing wind. Digestion is achieved by the energy of the fire-like wind.

The distribution of nutrition throughout the entire body, including the blood, cells, muscles, and organs, is through the action of the pervasive wind energy. Ultimately, the energy of food is able to support your very heartbeat and vitality through the movement of life-force energy.

The complicated processes of digestion could not take place at all

DESCRIPTIONS OF *LUNG* ENERGIES

LUNG	LOCATION	ELEMENT
upward moving wind	chest area, up through the nose and brain to the crown chakra	earth
life-force wind	heart and lung area	space
fire-like wind	upper abdomen, housing the stomach and intestines	fire
pervasive wind	entire body, especially the five limbs	wind
downward clearing wind	lower abdomen, housing the bladder, colon, and sexual organs	water

without the action and interaction of the five root *lung* energies. This is just one simple example of the critical role they play at the base of everything we are and do.

Depending upon whether an energy is in balance with the other energies or not, the effects of each *lung* can be positive or negative. Balanced *lung* energies support one another and help us to live healthy, joyful, and peaceful lives. When the energies are not balanced, we become sick, unhealthy, and unhappy. You can see why it is important to promote the greatest balance possible for all five root *lungs*.

The following tables summarize the basic character, function, and effects of the five root *lung* energies:

Color	Shape	Activity
yellow	umbrella with central shaft pushing up and holding out the spokes	breathing (inhalation/exhalation), swallowing, speaking; improves and clears the senses; purifies headaches, sore throat, and chest problems
white	diamond, or sparkling jewel, from the heart of the earth	brings life force, confidence, success, and fulfilment; clears the mind and heart
red	trident, like a three-pointed flaring fire	digestion/nutritional balance, temperature regulation, burns poison, purifies stomach problems, support and healing for the whole body
green	sun rays shining out everywhere	support and healing for the whole body, especially for the skin and muscles/joints of the five limbs
blue	bellows, with power to increase energy and push the wind	support for waste elimination and sexual function; support and healing for lower body (gas problems, etc.)

Consequences of Imbalances of *Lung*

Imbalanced *Lung*	Functional Losses
upward moving wind	difficulty or loss of speaking, diminished senses of the face
life-force wind	Shortened life due to a loss of life-force energy, heart problems, poor memory
fire-like wind	poor digestion and nutrition; related organ problems, especially stomach problems (gas, vomiting)
pervasive wind	skin problems; stiffness, lack of flexibility
downward clearing wind	lower abdominal problems, including those related to elimination and sexual function

Physical Diseases	Negative Emotions
brain problems (dizziness, headache, fainting, blindness, deafness)	harmful speech (lies, gossip, harsh words)
heart disease (panic attack, heart attack); insanity	anger (frustration, hatred, tantrums, rage, agitation)
organ problems, especially gall bladder;[6] swelling, edema	indolence (tiredness, heaviness, torpor); ignorance (confusion, indecision, wandering/scattered mind)
bone, joint, and muscle problems (pain, arthritis, stiffness); spleen problems	jealousy (envy, stealing, criticizing, judging)
kidney problems	desire (greedy, possessive, controlling, demanding); depression (disappointment, unmet expectations)

SPIRITUAL PRACTICES USING *LUNG*

LUNG	METHODS FOR FOCUSING ON *LUNG*	BENEFITS
upward moving wind	close nostrils and open crown chakra	opens crown chakra and liberates the mind
life-force wind	relax the mind and become gentle	brings long life; increases awareness, mindfulness, and memory
fire-like wind	hold stable, cross-legged posture (like the shore and basin of rock that holds the lake)	brings warmth of pleasure and peace; purifies sickness/disease
pervasive wind	move head and limbs toward each other (head slightly bent forward, legs together, hands together)	brings miracles and brings clarity to visions, signs, and dreams
downward clearing wind	tighten the perineum, closing the bottom doors	brings bliss/pleasure; clears and opens all of the channels

Spiritual Results	Paranormal Results
body becomes light, like a bird; brings greater joy and laughter; improves tone and resonance of the voice (for chanting)	the ability to experience a lighter physical body in feats related to floating, jumping, and flying; the ability to travel at another level (Pure Land, Buddha Land)
brings greater joy, rejuvenation, and vitality; brings greater awareness and clarity	the ability to control longevity and time of death; the ability, at death, to move consciousness/mind into another body (*phowa trong juk*)
increases feelings of warmth and pleasure; facilitates realization of emptiness	the ability to recognize clear light in the dream state, fearlessness, the tendency to be free of harm or obstacles presented by fire or water (for example, the ability to walk on fire or water without harm)
increases spiritual signs, symbolism; increases miracles/paraphenomena	the ability to manifest in many "untouchable" or nonphysical forms for the benefit of beings, as symbolized in the many arms/eyes of Shenlha Ödkar, the buddha of compassion (also known as Chenrezig in Tibetan or Avalokiteshvara in Sanskirt)
brings great bliss	the ability to reach the ultimate state of blissfulness and realization through the "desire" path (*chakpa lamkhyer*)—this is a disciplined practice of union that leads to liberation, not attachment

4. Middle and Lower Breath Exercises

When I am afraid, my breath is shallow.
When I am relaxed, my breath is deep.
When I am loved and cared for, breath is smiling at the heart.

THERE ARE THREE LEVELS of breathing: upper, middle, and lower breath. Upper breath is confined to the high chest area. It is shallow breathing that results in a poor air exchange for the body and a shallow, surface-level quality for the mind. People have a tendency to breathe like this if they are depressed, anxious, afraid, or stressed. Needless to say, there are no exercises here for the upper breath.

Middle breath is breathing into your heart and lung area. This breathing is good for your internal organs and will help to stabilize your mind.

Lower breath is breathing into your belly or below your navel. This is good for digestion and the lower organs. It is also good for the skin and the five senses.

Both the middle and lower levels of breathing can be used as methods for cleansing and balancing gross *lung*. They are used primarily to benefit the physical body.

Following are a few simple breathing exercises that can be learned quickly and easily.

MIDDLE BREATH PRACTICE

The middle breath exercise is done by visualizing and mindfully directing the breath into the area of the heart and lungs. It is a deeper style of breathing that is necessary for a strong, healthy heart and lungs.

There are three variations of middle breath practice. Repetitions help develop a familiarity with the middle breath. They also promote healing if the lungs are weak from birth or from disease, smoking, or other forms of air pollution.

MIDDLE BREATH EXERCISE #1

- ▸ Sit cross-legged on a meditation cushion or on a chair with your feet flat on the ground.
- ▸ Sit with your back straight, head slightly bent, and arms/hands in a comfortable position.
- ▸ Slowly and gently take a deep breath in through your nostrils.
- ▸ Imagine sending that breath into the area that holds your heart and lungs.
- ▸ Now exhale through the nostrils.
- ▸ Remember to inhale and exhale fully. In this exercise, you do not hold your breath in the heart area.
- ▸ Repeat nine times for one set and then take a short break.

The length of your break should be at least forty-five seconds or a few minutes. Use this time to relax and be aware of your body. You can do a total of three sets if you wish.

MIDDLE BREATH EXERCISE #2

Now do the same practice, but after inhaling fully, hold the breath as long as you can before releasing it. Complete repetitions and sets as in the first practice.

MIDDLE BREATH EXERCISE #3

Breathe in and out as fully as possible and much faster than normal breathing. This is a pumping action that you can hear and feel as the breath is being pulled in and pushed out.

Complete repetitions and sets as in the first practice.

LOWER BREATH PRACTICE

The lower breath is directed to the navel, or stomach area. It promotes general health, healing, and balance, and is particularly effective in reducing stress and negative emotions. Physically, the lower breath supports the liver, stomach, and kidneys.

The same three practice variations described for middle breath can be done for lower breath:

Lower Breath Exercise #1
Start with deep, relaxing breaths into the belly.

Lower Breath Exercise #2
Breathe in, hold the breath in the belly as long as possible, and release.

Lower Breath Exercise #3

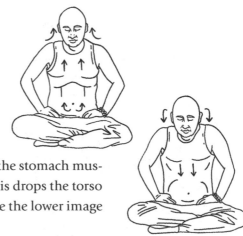

- ▸ Take rapid, pumping breaths directed in and out of the belly.
- ▸ As you exhale, squeeze the stomach muscles to push the breath out. This pushes the torso and shoulders up slightly. As you inhale, relax the stomach muscles and expand the belly. This drops the torso and shoulders back down (see the lower image on the right).

Lower Breath Exercise #4

- ► Start by sitting on a cushion or chair. Breathe in fully.

- ► Lean forward from the waist as far as possible with your forehead toward the ground. At the same time, squeeze your stomach muscles and expel as much air as possible through the nostrils.

- ► Keep squeezing your belly and holding your breath out while you sit up straight again.

- ► Relax, with your palms on your knees, and remain in this position for as long as possible.

- ► When you can no longer hold the breath out comfortably, slowly take a deep breath in through the nostrils.

- ► Repeat from three up to nine times for one set. You can do more sets if you feel comfortable. Remember to take a break between sets for at least forty-five seconds to rest your body in inner silence.

Note: Do not use force to hold the breath out. You should remain comfortable and not stressed or in pain. Holding the breath out for too long is not helpful and could cause more harm than good, especially for beginners.

HEALING WITH MIDDLE AND LOWER BREATH

As a daily practice, middle and lower breath exercises are very helpful for people suffering from a variety of conditions, such as asthma, organ problems, stomach upsets, or indigestion.

I know of many Tibetans now living in southern India who have had health problems due to the change of climate and culture from Tibet. They used the middle breath practice to increase their *lung* function and general health.

One of my friends is a living example of how powerful middle and lower breathing practice can be. As with many other Tibetans who escaped to India, he became very ill. He could not sleep or eat in the heat and suffered from severe digestive problems. I was afraid he might die. He tried pills and herbal medicines. He went to Tibetan doctors and Western doctors. Nothing helped, and he became weaker and weaker over the years.

Finally, he decided to focus on middle and lower breath exercises along with *tsa lung* movements.[7] His daily practice included the pumping, middle, and lower breath exercises that he did in sets of hundreds, up to thousands of times, three times a day for one year. He also did a bit of the lower breath practice, holding the breath out. Slowly his muscles and body became stronger. His stomach healed and he was able to eat and digest his food. When I saw him a number of years later, I didn't recognize him. The transformation was amazing. For him, these exercises proved to be the best medicine.

The international popularity of Indian yoga and Chinese qigong has led to an ever-increasing interest in energy-related practices, including the ones described here. For many generations in Tibet, these practices were kept secret. Today, the secrecy has been lifted and the exercises are being used by more and more people for health and healing.

I encourage you to use these simple exercises every day, not just when you are ill, stressed, or are having emotional difficulties. As with anything else in life, the more you do the exercises, the more comfortable you will be with them. Enter the practice and relax. Release any tension that has built up and feel what is left: inner peace. This is the place of healing and health.

PART II

The Healing Power of Breath

5: The Meaning of Healing

Breath is the supporter who cares for me.
Breath is the protector who gives me strength.
Breath is the teacher who gives me courage.
Breath is the silence that brings calm and peace.
Breath is the medicine that heals when I hurt.
Breath is the mother who gives birth and life.
Breath is the path of enlightenment and compassion.

HEALING IS RESTORING the balance and flow of *lung* energy. It is a return to well-being.

In the background of every moment, we are healing through spontaneous processes of repair and rejuvenation that are constantly taking place in all of our tissues, organs, and biological systems.

We can also heal in very obvious and dramatic ways after experiencing significant energy loss or damage through disturbances such as disease, injury, trauma, or emotional pain.

Well-being comes from stable, vibrant connections between our body, mind, and soul and between ourselves, others, and the environment. Healing is reconnecting with what has been lost, damaged, or disconnected.

The most important connection to honor is the one with our deepest, most authentic self. Every spiritual tradition has a way of encouraging followers to know and be true to themselves. A "disconnect" at this level manifests in many forms of dis-ease, unhappiness, and mental instability.

Our health and energy are carried on our breath. It is like a bridge connecting us with what is most important. This is "the healing power of breath."

HEALING OR CURING?

Healing is becoming whole or complete again after a period of trouble caused by energetic blockage or disruption. It is recovering from the trouble by returning to a state of equilibrium.

Curing, on the other hand, is the end of all symptoms related to a specific physical or mental challenge. Curing may be a part of healing but that is not always so. Someone may be healed but not cured and someone may be cured but not healed.

For example, no matter how strong and healthy you are right now, you will eventually die. Your body will dissolve and go back to mother earth. Dying is a most important time for healing and, obviously, not a time for curing or restoring the physical body.

The underlying foundation of health or illness is the mind. The highest fulfillment of being and healing occurs when the mind is calm, clear, and at rest in its natural state of primordial awareness. This is the Dzogchen view, which is called "the great perfection" or "the great completion." It is coming to understand and rest in the fullness of who we really are.

WE ARE ENERGY

Energy is what we are. Unfortunately, we often completely forget this fact and focus primarily on the outer form of our body—on what we look like and what we do.

As physical, spiritual beings, we are a complex network of energy moving throughout our body, speech, and mind. It moves as every action and interaction, as everything we think and say, and as every breath and heartbeat.

Energy moves along unseen pathways within, called *tsa*, and along visible pathways such as our nerves. It moves within every organ and physical system of the body and as an overall matrix or vibrational field that is perceptible and can be measured with instruments.

In general, when *lung* is balanced and pure it is called *positive*. Positive energy flows in accordance with our essential nature, resulting in the experience of well-being. It is linked to the ever-renewing and refreshing qualities of the four immeasurables: joy, love, compassion, and equanimity.

Lung is called *negative* when it is imbalanced or contaminated, especially by the classic five poisons of the mind:

- ▸ Ignorance: confusion, delusion, not understanding reality or oneself
- ▸ Aversion: anger, hatred, avoidance
- ▸ Attachment: grasping, holding, greed, desire, selfishness
- ▸ Jealousy: envy, discontent
- ▸ Pride: arrogance, conceit

We can choose to carry positive energy and be well. To do this, we must become aware of what nurtures energetic balance and what interferes with or obstructs it.

Healing is moving from negative to positive energy. With intention and practice, we can choose to heal and be well in every moment.

ENVIRONMENTAL REVIEW

The problems and disturbances we experience in life always arise out of specific causes and conditions. They are a product of what we call *karma*, the endless cycle of cause and effect. For example, if the nature of our thinking, speaking, and action is negative, it will cause negative results that are experienced as suffering for ourselves and others.

The suffering may range from low-level, subconscious mental struggles to acute, life-threatening diseases.

The first thing a doctor tries to discover when observing the symptoms of a sick patient is the cause of those symptoms. Then an effective course of action or medicine can be prescribed.

The same is true for our own healing. Understanding the causes of our physical and mental suffering is the first step in the healing process. In the Tibetan view, this investigation begins with a look at the physical, emotional, and social environments we are living in.

Physical Environment

Our outer, physical environment is a fine balance of the five elements: space, wind or air, fire, water, and earth. They are the source of all phenomena in the universe. At the subtlest level they are five luminous, primordial energies from which all others emerge. Each one of them has inherent qualities and energy that can be called the spirit of that element. Because we are not separate from our environment and its spirit, when we disturb the health of that spirit around us, we will disturb our own health.

We are literally made of the food we eat, the water we drink, and the air we breathe. Polluting space is polluting our mind because our consciousness is connected to the external space element. Polluting water is polluting our blood because our blood is connected to the external water element. Polluting air is polluting our breath and mind or consciousness since they are connected to the outer air or wind element. Polluting fire is polluting our own internal heat, digestion, and life-energy because all of these are connected to the outer fire element.

Emotional Environment

The health of our body and mind is also linked to our emotional environment. The five poisons of the mind destroy health. Anger, for example, is extremely disrupting. You may think you can direct it at someone else, but it always harms you yourself from the inside out. Likewise, resentment held in the heart can destroy your entire body and mental state. Negative thoughts directed toward yourself or others can pollute your mind and become the seed of illness.

SOCIAL ENVIRONMENT

The third aspect of our environment is social. When the people around you are peaceful, gentle, and caring, they create a social environment that will affect your life in a beneficial way. If your community, family, and friends tend to be negative and violent, you will most likely be affected by their negative energy and lifestyle.

I remember one of my students who, after taking the refuge ceremony and ritual from me, seemed happy and fully engaged with his mind and heart in the spiritual life. At that time, he had just moved to the city where my center is. Unfortunately, the work environment at his new job was full of negativity, anger, and violence.

I saw him change into a dissatisfied, unhappy, unenergetic, depressed person who found it very difficult to keep up with the everyday challenges at work. This is a perfect example of how important the social and work environment is to each of us, and how easy it is for family members, colleagues, or partners to affect the lives around them.

When any part of our environment becomes damaged or unstable, it is easy to sit back and criticize or blame others. It's also easy to wait for someone else to deal with the problems. But the first step toward change should be your own.

For example, imagine five family members living together in one house. If each one waits for someone else to start caring for and cleaning up the house, no one will take action. The living environment will soon become an unhealthy mess for all of them. But if, instead of waiting, even one person takes some action and responsibility, the others will follow the example.

Taking action to care for your emotional, physical, and social environment will improve conditions for yourself and those around you. This is true whether we are talking about your own household, your own town, or the entire global village.

THE MOST POWERFUL MEDICINE

Although there are many things we can do to assist healing, the most important thing is to regularly stop and do nothing. Just be quiet, physically stay still, and mentally let go.

Doing nothing may seem like the hardest thing to do, but once we get past the habitual pressure to always do something, sitting calmly with things just as they are can become the most powerful medicine we choose to take.

Within this quiet space healing can begin by simply recognizing any physical, emotional, or mental disturbances. The approach should be one of gentle, nonjudgmental inquiry. "What's going on? Why do I feel like this? When did this struggle start? Where did it come from?"

Such an investigation requires serious contemplation. If we're just dancing on the surface or poking around intellectually, we will not achieve the realization needed to open the doors to healing.

We need to be willing to work at this: to become sensitive to the real issues, to be sure we're seeing clearly, and to go deeper, as required.

Very often, people just don't want to go there, especially if their underlying problems seem too big or frightening to deal with. In such cases, seeking help from a trusted friend, doctor, therapist, or spiritual teacher is a good next step.

When we can acknowledge and understand our afflictions, healing can be faster and easier. This is a fundamental part of taking responsibility for our own health and well-being.

GETTING TO THE BOTTOM OF THINGS

One exercise I highly recommend for understanding your own struggles and energetic imbalances is taking the time to review past events and circumstances for clues about what might be obstructing you.

During such a review, while trying to write my life story, I was able to fully acknowledge all the loss, hurt, and trauma I had suffered as a child in Tibet. Of most significance was the sudden death of my mother when I was only six years old. No one explained to me what had happened or offered me any comfort. I was left with my own intense feelings of being abandoned and somehow to blame.

There were many other trials that followed, including periods of hunger and poverty, having to stay with different relatives, being beaten for my mistakes, and being left alone in the wilderness for extended periods to protect a large herd of sheep.

As I recalled these events, I came to realize that I wasn't really happy. In some ways, I had become stuck. My early feelings of insecurity and fear after my mother's death were still playing out in subtle ways, such as the drive I felt to always please, to always do better, to always search for something outside myself. I wept for hours.

Through the tears, I was able to clearly see and finally come to terms with those childhood traumas. I was able to overcome my underlying feelings of loss and sadness and find closure. At the same time, I also came to recognize who I really am now and acknowledge with appreciation my gifts, good qualities, and accomplishments. I finally felt complete and fully at ease. I was healed.

Expressing your experiences in writing can play a significant role in healing. You might think, as I did at first, that there isn't much to write about. Trust me, that isn't true. Everyone has a precious life journey. I encourage you to pick up the pen, pay attention, and see what happens.

HEALING IS FREEDOM

Healing is freedom from struggles. These struggles can manifest as energetic disturbances on three seemingly different but completely interdependent levels: external, internal, and secret, or less obvious.

External struggles include problems with our relationship to the outer world. A disturbance or loss of what Tibetans called *wang tang* (prosperity) energy results in an interference with our ability to thrive and prosper. Disturbances of what they call *lung ta* (reputation) energy disrupts our relationships and interactions with others, resulting in damage to our reputation.

Internal struggles are related to the loss or damage of *lu* (health) energy. This results in problems with the physical body such as illness and injury.

Secret struggles have to do with mental afflictions, including negative emotions such as anger, jealousy, depression, and attachment. They are the most subtle and difficult of challenges, arising from the loss or disruption of *la* (soul or spirit) energy—the energy of our deepest level of existence, which make us, to a large degree, who we are.

SOUL RETRIEVAL

My Bön tradition is the oldest indigenous spiritual tradition of the Himalayan region. The nine vehicles it presents for spiritual growth go from ancient shamanic rituals intended to dispel obstacles appearing as external forces to the highest levels of realization in nondual pristine awareness.

In the older shamanic view, the main focus for healing is the soul. In the ancient texts, *la* is described as being in relationship to our consciousness (*yi*) and our mind (*sem*). The condition of our soul determines the condition of the other two. If our soul is strong and stable, so will our consciousness and mind be strong and stable.

Soul loss leads to a loss of mental confidence and stability. It also leads to a loss of *sog*, or life-force energy. *La* and *sog* can be nurtured and rejuvenated. Tibetans believe they can also be damaged, lost, or stolen through trauma or by other entities.

The shamanic soul and life-force retrieval ceremonies, called Laguk and Tseguk, are done regularly in Tibet to restore someone's physical, mental, and spiritual health as well as restore harmony to the surrounding environment and the entire universe.

Every summer, my cousin goes into the nomadic territory of northeastern Tibet and, as a ritual master, is able to partake in these retrieval ceremonies. Many times he has witnessed the complete healing of individuals who had tried all manner of other treatments unsuccessfully.

The soul retrieval ritual includes an offering made to acknowledge and satisfy the underlying need or cause of the illness. The source of affliction is understood to be in relationship with the patient and is approached through a kind of respectful dialogue or negotiation. It is seen as feeding on the patient's health and is directed to stop and replace that diet with what is being offered symbolically and in good faith.

In the visualized presence of the Buddha of Longevity, Tsewang Rigdzin, apologies are made by the patient for anything he or she may have done to cause the disturbance. Instead of fighting an enemy, the process is more like waging peace by seeking harmony through an agreement that will leave both parties satisfied.

The method is compassion; the goal is peace; the result is freedom.

APPROACHES TO HEALING

There is a basic difference between the standard Western and Tibetan medical approaches to healing. Consider the analogy of disease as a thief that has come to steal pleasure and well-being.

In Western medicine, the usual response is to immediately terminate the thief or stop it by locking all the gates, doors, and windows.

Although this approach is extremely effective for conditions such as a broken leg or appendicitis, it often fails to address underlying sources that may exist for conditions such as depression, cancer, or diabetes.

In Tibetan medicine, the understanding is that the thief is already in, so the first response is to examine the intruder: "Where did you come from? Why do you want to steal? What is it that you need? Are you angry about something? Have you been hurt?"

The focus is to find and transform the thief. Although this process may appear to take longer, it can be more effective. By addressing the thief, the root causes of the problem are addressed and the gates of healing can naturally swing open.

THE BEST ATTITUDE

The best attitude for healing is to be open, compassionate, humble, and responsive. There may be a million reasons, causes, and conditions that have given rise to an affliction. Be open to that. Not everything is in your control and not everything is your fault. Just do your best and let go. Give the process some space.

We don't always know what the best or highest good might be for us at any particular time. Often, instead of fighting, it's not until we let go fully that things can shift. We may need to go through difficulties, illness, or injury as a critical part of our spiritual growth. Instead of focusing on a particular outcome, learn to trust in the power and potential of the healing process itself.

Expectation can close opportunities and possibilities and become a huge obstacle to healing. Grasping for a cure or some other particular future goal can blind us to what we really need right now.

For example, if I feel I need to meet someone in my life and walk directly toward where I think that person should be, I may be brushing past who I really need to see on the way.

The best approach to healing is what I call "50/50." There is a 50 percent chance that, for example, my medication, therapy, or spiritual practice might lead to healing, and there's a 50 percent chance that it might not. This light, relaxed, open invitation to the healing process is a perfectly balanced approach.

Remember to be patient. Afflictions may have taken a long time to manifest, and they may take some time to disarm.

COMBINING HEALING METHODS

Any kind of energy that is weak or imbalanced can be restored through different healing methods, including medical, psychological, or spiritual treatments. These different healing modalities can be combined for the best outcome. For example, a cancer patient may have surgery, opt for chemotherapy, see a psychiatrist or counsellor, and do daily healing meditation practices using the breath.

I often tell my students, if they are taking medication, to see it as a symbol of healing and say a prayer or healing mantra first, then take a breath with healing intention and blow it over the pills. Focusing the breath, the mind, and the emotions in this way is energetically beneficial and will assist the healing process.

This kind of approach is similar to the careful way Tibetans take special, precious pills. They are made of seventy different minerals and herbs and are taken by someone to promote health, whether the person is sick or not.

For three days before and after taking the pill, food intake is restricted and simplified. Before going to bed on the evening the pill is to be taken, it is smashed into a powder, mixed with water in a special, unblemished bowl, and covered with a blue silk cloth. The person then goes to sleep, awakes before the light of early morning, visualizes Menlha, the medicine buddha, in front of them, unifies with the Buddha, drinks the mixture, and then goes back to sleep to rest and digest the medicine.

This practice shows how healing can be honored as a sacred process and how treatment can be approached with reverence and imagination through ritual. This kind of combination can lead to amazing results.

6. Riding the Breath

Breath is a horse
that carries the mind
along paths of inner light and healing,
headed home to the Palace of Peace.

UNDERSTANDING THE RELATIONSHIP of mind and *lung* energy is critical for healing and maintaining our physical and mental well-being. The Tibetan view in this regard is extremely helpful. The three key words of energy dynamics according to this view are *tsa, lung,* and *tigle.*

Tsa refers to the energy channel. *Lung,* in this case, refers to the movement of inner air or vital energy. *Tigle* refers to the mind or the clear-light quality of the nature of mind.

These three are likened to a path (energy channel), a horse (energy), and the rider of the horse (mind). If you want to go somewhere, it is easy to get there when all three are together. If there is no road or horse, it is very difficult to walk by yourself.

For a modern analogy, think of a road, a car, and a driver. Again, if you have all three, the journey is easy. If the car or the road is missing, you may never get where you want to go.

Now, consider healing to be the place you want to go. If we can fully enter the present moment, focus the mind, and stay in the saddle, we can heal ourselves.

SIMPLE HEALING EXERCISES

Right now, just relax and become aware of your breathing. Simply notice any sensations of the breath coming in and going out, such as coolness or dryness as it comes in through the nostrils, warmth or movement as it passes over the lip, and in general any changes or differences in inhalation or exhalation. If the mind wanders and other thoughts come up, just release them and refocus the mind. Bring it home to the breath, again and again.

In time, the body will relax, the mind will become clear, and energy will start to shift and move in response. Now, horse and rider can go places.

Consider, for example, you want to assist the healing of an injury or arthritis in your right knee. Relax and bring the mind home, as described. Now follow these simple steps for riding the breath toward self-healing:

- ► Take a slow, deep breath and gently hold it in. As you inhale, imagine healing light flooding into your body with the breath.
- ► As you hold the breath, imagine moving it and the light to your right knee, then take some time and imagine radiating that healing light throughout your knee.
- ► When you are ready, release the breath and imagine any pain or soreness being released with it.
- ► The area of pain or damage is like a house full of smoke. This breathing practice is like opening all the doors and windows, letting light and fresh air in and letting the smoke out. Do it as often as you like and as long as you feel the need. Be patient and trust that, over time, this kind of care and attention will be healing.

Unifying mind, breath, and light in this kind of exercise is a powerful healing tool that is physically, psychologically, and energetically beneficial.

HEALING MANTRAS

In the example above, healing energy is generated by being mindful of the breath linked to a sense of light. With mantras, healing energy is generated by being mindful of the breath linked to a sense of sound that is voiced on the out-breath.

A mantra may be a word, a group of words, or a sacred syllable or sound. Repeating or reciting healing mantras with the correct intention generates healing energy.

In my Tibetan culture, healing practices always include mantra recitations. A mantra session starts with setting the intention to bring the highest good or benefit to one and all. The selected mantra is then said or sung three, seven, twenty-one, or more times.

The session ends with a special breath of blessing. This is done by blowing your own breath up into your nostrils, directing it there with your lower lip. You then inhale that as a blessing for your whole body and mind and for any particular place of struggle or pain. As you inhale, imagine your body becoming luminous with the breath. You are radiating light. As you breathe out, visualize blowing the blessing as healing white light to all beings, especially those people you know need help and healing. If you are thinking of or attending to someone in particular, it can be directed to them in a general way or to any specific area of pain or discomfort they may be having.

Mantras are described in more detail in part 6, "Breath and Sound."

WIND HORSE

Our physical breath moves inseparably with the movement of *lung*, linking the energies of our body and mind. When we relax our body and become aware of our breath, allowing it to settle into a steady rhythm, our mind will also settle. The mind can then ride the breath like a horse, directing vital energy in amazing ways.

These concepts are captured beautifully in the Tibetan image for *lung ta*, the wind horse. This mythical creature symbolizes our own vitality. With great power, it rises up on the wind, carrying and delivering energy, prayers, healing, balance, and good fortune to all those in need.

At any time, in any place, we can practice mindfulness of breathing, connecting the horse and rider. The simple, life-giving movement of air in and out of our body is a constant invitation to use our mind and guide the horse.

7. The Healing Practice of Tonglen

When need arises
and you have the ability,
opportunity is your gift.

Take it without waiting
or thinking too much.

Breath in and receive,
breath out and give.

The more you give,
the more you will receive—
this is a natural law of life.

TONGLEN IS TIBETAN for "giving and taking" or "sending and receiving." It is a healing method that uses breath and the imagination to take in and transform the suffering of others while sending or giving them whatever is needed for their highest good. It is a simple but powerful practice of healing and compassion in the face of suffering.

Basically, the practice involves breathing in and receiving another's pain, feeling it transform into light within the heart, then breathing out and sending the light of happiness and relief to the one who is suffering. This is recycling at its best.

This practice is often described as "exchanging self for other." It is putting yourself in another's shoes, exchanging your benefit for their difficulty, exchanging positive energy for negative energy.

Tonglen can be done for anyone who is suffering, ill, in pain, or dying. It can also be done for yourself or applied in a more general way for the environment and the natural world.

This practice is a direct antidote to the very common feeling of helplessness we often experience when we or those around us are caught in the grip of sickness, suffering, or death. It is something very practical that we can do to remain present, calm, compassionate, and open in otherwise difficult and awkward times.

Typically, we respond to pain and suffering with resistance, blame, self-focus, and reliance on others to explain or solve our problems. We tend to forget the resources we have within us.

Tonglen turns the usual approach on its head. Instead of breathing in all that is bright and wonderful and getting rid of darkness and pain, we face the darkness and receive it with the intention of transforming it, and we give what is most valued and helpful.

This process tames the ego, moving us away from self-focus. At the same time, it generates a loving connection and confidence in the power of compassionate intention.

As with compassion training in general, tonglen is traditionally taught in stages that gradually break down the habitual tendencies of the ego to fixate on "me" and "mine." Practice begins with oneself, moves to loved ones, then to others—including unknown, difficult, or harmful individuals—and, eventually, to anyone and everyone.

The following are the three basic progressive steps for developing the healing power of tonglen.

STEP 1: TONGLEN FOR YOURSELF

In the sending and receiving practice of tonglen, it is very important that you start with yourself. If you cannot exercise compassion for yourself in this way, how can you think of trying to do the same for another?

Practicing tonglen to restore your own balance and integrity will help you to recognize and respect your own innate resources and potential for healing.

- Visualize yourself sitting in front of you, like your reflection in a mirror.
- Take time to notice any tension, discomfort, imbalance, stress, or bad feelings in your reflection. Imagine any negative energy there as darkness within your reflection, like dark clouds.
- Set your intention to release the darkness and be free from negative energy.
- Breathe in through your nostrils and hold the breath. As you inhale, imagine sucking all the darkness out of your reflection from the top of its head, in through your nostrils, down the central energy channel, and into your heart.
- Imagine the darkness immediately transforming there into pure, white light. This is powerful medicine and the most important moment of the practice.
- When you are ready, gently blow out through your lips, sending healing light to your reflection, where it enters the top of its head and fills the entire body.
- Now unify or merge with your reflection. Feel the light radiating within you, like an enlightened being. Feel the joy, freedom, and renewal of this sacred practice.
- Repeat the process as many times as you like, until you feel some sense of healing, comfort, and/or renewal.

STEP 2: TONGLEN FOR LOVED ONES

Once you are comfortable practicing tonglen for yourself, try doing it for a loved one, or someone you know:

- Sit with a loved one or someone you know, or visualize that person in front of you.
- Take time to recognize any struggles or pain the person may be having. See it on the face, in the body, or all around the person.
- With tremendous compassion, see yourself as someone with

the energy, confidence, and ability to help relieve his or her suffering.

▸ Breathe in through your nostrils and hold the breath. As you inhale, imagine all the darkness and negative energy from within your loved one leaving from the top of his or her head, entering your nostrils, and moving down the central energy channel into your heart.

▸ Imagine the darkness transforming there into pure, white light.

▸ When you are ready, gently blow out through your lips, sending healing light to the top of your loved one's head where it enters and fills the person's body, fully restoring balance. If you have visualized someone, imagine the smile of joy and relief on their face; imagine that their mood and the energy in and around them has changed; imagine their gratitude for your help and support.

STEP 3: TONGLEN FOR EVERYONE

In this next step of developing compassion, you start moving out of the comfort zone of your "tribe" by practicing for those you don't know, for whom you feel neutral. Maybe it's a person you've seen on the street or someone you've heard about on the radio.

Normally, we don't really pay attention to strangers. We seem to need reasons to open our heart to them in the same way we automatically do with family and friends.

For example, you might knock on someone's door, and an elderly woman answers. A typical, dismissive first impression might be something like, "Oh, this is just an old lady," as though the person's value had diminished with time.

Then, she invites you in for a moment. As you look around, you see the story of her life portrayed in photos of her childhood, education, family, loved ones, and accomplishments.

Knowing her story suddenly shifts your perception of her as just some old lady; you start to see her as a whole person who experiences the joys and sorrows of life, just like you, and deserves to be treated with honor, respect, and compassion.

Tonglen will help you remember that everyone has a story. You don't need to know the details behind every life to justify releasing your loving kindness. Just do it.

After you've gained some experience practicing for those with whom you have no emotional ties, try practicing for those you are tied to through negative emotion. These are the ones who may be your enemy, who bother you or have a way of "pushing your buttons."

Remember, there are always reasons behind someone's negative, annoying, or destructive behavior. Instead of reacting to it with hostility, remain steady and ready to recycle negative energy through the transformative power of tonglen.

Eventually, you won't hesitate to send help in this way to anyone in need. With great compassion, your desire and practice will be for all living beings, equally, as described here:

▸ Visualize the suffering of individuals, communities, the world, or the entire universe.
▸ Take time to see the struggles and the suffering.
▸ Set a big intention: Imagine yourself to be an enlightened being, full of compassion, strength, and confidence that you can relieve the suffering of all beings.
▸ Breathe in through your nostrils and hold the breath. As you inhale, imagine taking in a dark cloud of collective pain and suffering from all beings.
▸ As you hold the breath, imagine that when the cloud reaches your heart it is transformed into magnificent healing light.
▸ When you are ready, release the breath while imagining millions of rays of light being released at the same time, traveling to all those in need, relieving them and making the world a better place to live.

UNCONDITIONAL LOVE

Tonglen is a practice of unconditional love. Don't make it conditional by expecting a cure or looking for results. Just do the practice with an open heart and let go. As in the 50/50 attitude I mentioned above, it may help physically and it may not.

When someone asks me to pray for them, I do so wholeheartedly, trusting it will help in some way—if not now, then maybe sometime in the future. I do this without expectation and without excitation or disappointment if results are evident or not.

A beloved Tibetan story of unconditional love and compassion involves a spiritual master who was walking through western Tibet on a pilgrimage with a few of his students.

They came to the crossing place of a wide, fast-flowing river and found an old lady who had been waiting for a long time to cross, as no one would help her.

As they approached, they could see she had leprosy and discussed what should be done. Usually, should a spiritual teacher decide to help someone, he or she would tell their students to go to the person's aid. But this master told the students he would help the woman himself by carrying her across the river on his back.

The master introduced himself to the woman. He could see the suffering on her face. He could see the spirit of disease within her and how it was feeding on her body. The master was filled with compassion and wanted to help not just the lady, but the spirit as well.

He carried the woman across the river and then, with every breath, took her suffering into himself and let her go completely free. He took in the spirit of the disease but wasn't worried in the least. His spiritual practice was the most important thing to him, and he knew this disease would not interfere with it at all.

The students could see that their master had come down with leprosy and insisted on getting rid of it. But the master didn't want to reject the spirit. He sent his students home, found a cave to retreat in, and happily continued with his meditation.

One day a spider, representing the disease, tried to come out of his left nostril. The master pushed it back in and insisted it should stay on and be happy.

Eventually, the spider emerged and confessed it was extremely unhappy. The master's tremendous compassion of tonglen was not the kind of food it found delicious. It normally thrived in an environment of anger, fighting, frustration, anxiety, and fear of death.

The master said he would not fight with the spirit. If it wasn't happy, he would let it go on the condition that it would no longer wander in samsara, chasing down and infecting others. It was time to liberate its consciousness, which, with the help of the master, immediately transformed into enlightenment.

Like the master, our capacity for compassion has the power to bring about our highest intention: to liberate ourselves and others.

IT'S ALL IN THE MIND

All perception is in the mind. As we saw, our first careless impression of an old lady can completely change when we consider her life and our shared experiences. The lady didn't change in the slightest; the change was all in the mind of the beholder.

Your perception of yourself or anyone else can change depending on your mindset. It's very important to understand what kind of view or filter your mind is bringing to how you perceive and understand things—and that you have a choice in the matter.

Some have a concern, when learning tonglen, that they might get stuck with the disease or condition of another person. However, the healing power of the mind in this practice is generated from the clear intention to recycle; to transform the negative energy received into the positive energy given. This mindset does not leave room for fearful imaginings of energy blockages or loss. It is placing one's courage and trust in the transformative power of love to help dispel another's physical or mental struggle.

You can see such struggles all the time in the news and on television.

Observe them with curiosity, patience, and equanimity, not with emotional involvement. Instead of sitting at home and becoming negative or depressed by what you see, keep positive energy flowing by practicing tonglen. Take the struggles you are witnessing and transform them in your heart. Breathe out spiritual healing for the world and all those who are suffering.

If you can't help becoming angry or anxious while watching the news, you should probably turn the TV off.

As you become familiar with the three steps for practicing tonglen, you will come to know what you are comfortable with and capable of. Don't force yourself to work with people or situations that make you feel unstable. Tonglen is meant to be a natural and spontaneous extension of love, like that of a mother for her child. It is up to you to choose the practice level and pace for reducing your ego and expanding your compassion and loving-kindness.

PART III

Breath and Meditation

8. Meditation and the Mind

Meditation creates an
outer and inner environment of
peace and harmony that is
necessary to connect to
your true home—your true self—
which is right here,
right now.

THE MAIN PURPOSE of meditation is to wake up and discover who we are. Who we are is beyond what we think we are or appear to be. Our most authentic essence is known as our buddha nature, or true nature of mind. It can only be discovered through meditation.

We usually wander lost in our thoughts and emotions, day after day and life after life. The cycles of difficulty and suffering that mark our existence come from not knowing the true nature of our mind.

AWAKENING FROM IGNORANCE

The inability to recognize the true nature of our mind and how thoughts arise and dissipate is an underlying ignorance called *marigpa*. This ignorance is not stupidity but a kind of ignoring or not seeing things as they are. It distracts our awareness like a cloud covering the sun in the blue sky. It manifests as negative *lung* that results in various forms of mental and physical suffering.

Another type of ignorance is ignoring or not seeing the causes and effects of suffering and happiness. If you asked someone if they want to be happy, they would say yes. If you asked someone if they want to suffer, they would say no. But if you asked what the causes of happiness and suffering are, they probably could not answer because of the ignorance of not knowing.

The Tibetan word for someone who has fully awakened from the sleep of ignorance is *sang gye*. *Sang* means "awakened from affliction" and *gye* means "complete wisdom."

The Sanskrit word for an awakened or enlightened one is *buddha*, which comes from the root word *bodhi*, meaning "awakening." If you add *citta* to that—from the root word *cit*, "that which is conscious"— you get the well-known word *bodhicitta*, translated as "awakening mind" or "mind of enlightenment."

Bodhicitta, the awakening mind, is a mind of great compassion that is always coupled with the intention and yearning to attain enlightenment in order to help others do the same.

Meditation is the tried and true way to the perfect wisdom and the limitless love, compassion, joy, and equanimity of a *sang gye*.

MIND AND THE NATURE OF MIND

The closest term for meditation in the Tibetan language is *gom*, which means "to become familiar." This accurately points to meditation as a process of becoming more and more familiar with the state of our mind and the principles of suffering, happiness, and transformation.

The mind we are all familiar with is called *sem* mind or the ego state of mind. This is the mind of thoughts, concepts, judgments, emotions, memories, and images. It is dualistic in nature because it operates by identifying subject and object, me or them, mine or theirs. It is in constant motion, grasping, desiring, fearing, or pushing away. It tends to travel away from the present moment and wander in either the past or the future. This is where the ego lives!

The ultimate nature of mind, known as *rigpa* or the natural state of mind, is a pure, nondual awareness and clarity that lies beyond the *sem* mind and has an unlimited ability to manifest. It is the state of being aware and fully present, beyond emotions, ego, and thoughts. It is a state of total peace. It is difficult to understand if you have never had a direct experience of it. This is the mind of living in the present moment without any attachment to the past or the future.

There are two ways humans can reach an understanding of anything. One is through conceptual, or intellectual, thinking. The other is through direct understanding, similar to what we may call an "aha!" moment. With direct understanding, no one has to explain or teach; there is no need for thoughts, concepts, or ideas. Direct experience produces a profound understanding that is beyond words. When you have direct experience, you just know it.

Direct, personal experience is the only way to know rigpa. It is impossible for a teacher to explain or teach exactly what the natural state of the mind is. It is like someone trying to explain to you what a particular candy tastes like. If you have never tasted that kind of candy, you will never know what it actually tastes like. Someone can describe their own perceptions of its color and shape and mention other foods that have a similar taste, but the actual taste is for you to discover for yourself.

The bottom line is that the ordinary, thinking mind cannot see itself or what is beyond itself. In the Dzogchen tradition they say, "A knife cannot cut itself" and "Blood cannot be washed away by blood." Only rigpa, the natural state of mind, can discover what is beyond the thinking mind. Only rigpa can see itself. We can come to experience this directly as *rigpé yeshé* or the "primordial awareness" that is the natural state of mind.

The state of rigpa is beyond ego and attachment. It is a clear, total, and complete awareness in the present moment—a oneness with the universe. It is not sitting quietly and relaxing for a few seconds with no thoughts, and it isn't falling asleep! It is not daydreaming, or chanting, or focusing on an object. Discovering this state of mind takes time, familiarity, and a complete release of any attachment to outcomes or goals.

When we are aware and recognize where thoughts originate, they will effortlessly liberate themselves back into the space or emptiness they appeared from.

What remains is positive *lung* energy with all of its related good qualities, such as love, joy, compassion, and equanimity.

TRAINING THE MIND

Mindfulness and awareness are two essential tools that are used together in meditation to train the mind. If you aren't using them, you aren't meditating.

Drenpa, the Tibetan word for mindfulness, literally means "remember." Remember what? Remember to be in the present moment. Mindfulness is something that is done with intention and effort. It is a choice to let go and fully enter the present moment in an open, unattached, and nonjudgmental way. Typically, the practice for achieving this is placing the mind's full attention on one object using one of the six senses: seeing, hearing, tasting, smelling, feeling, or thinking.

Normally, the mind is scattered, with all of the senses operating at the same time. It is like a water pipe unable to deliver a full load because of leakage out of five other holes along the way. Placing full attention on only one sense at a time is like a water pipe in excellent condition with only one opening at the end, delivering the full capacity and potential of the mind.

Awareness and mindfulness are similar in many respects but there is a subtle difference. Awareness is not doing but being. Being what? Being watchful. It operates in the background of every moment, observing everything. While mindfulness is being fully present with one thing, such as seeing, hearing, tasting, feeling, or thinking, awareness is the knowing that you are seeing, hearing, tasting, feeling, or thinking, along with anything else that may be occurring.

Awareness is a kind of vigilance. It is like a supervisor overseeing a trainee. It is always there but only seems to make itself known from time to time, standing there, overseeing the worker and the work.

Is he doing what he learned to do, or making a mistake, or doing something else altogether? Is she paying attention to the task or is she distracted, spaced out, or wandering off?

HABITS

One of the biggest problems with an untrained mind is its habitual tendency to get stuck in the past with what has already come and gone or fixate on some projected future that may or may not ever happen. Both are delusional states that, if left unchecked, can lead to extremely disturbing and painful conditions, such as depression and anxiety.

To some extent, we need to think about the past and plan for the future, but the only place we can live our lives is in the present moment. Mindfulness and awareness are right now. Training in them helps us let go of the past and future and connect fully to life as it is, moment by moment.

Many of the other habits of an untrained mind make it seem like a wild animal. In the extremes, it can be as jumpy and out of control as a monkey or as heavy and unmovable as a stubborn elephant. In order to tame and train them you need two tools: mindfulness and awareness.

Mindfulness is like a hook or a leash to pull in the wild monkey and keep it from racing around. Awareness is like a stick or a whip to push or inspire the elephant to get up and get moving.

Eventually, through using these tools again and again over time, both animals will learn how to obey and where to go to be happy. You will become their best friend and they will become yours. All aspects of the mind will become stable, content, and able to cooperate together to achieve whatever goal you set.

THE HANDLER

Mindfulness and awareness are wonderful tools, but in the hands of a bad trainer even the best tools are useless.

The mind, like the monkey and the elephant, will best respond to a handler who has attractive qualities that they can come to know, trust, and look forward to.

To effectively train your own mind, it is extremely important to be open and nonjudgmental. As a trainer, you should be loving, patient, and compassionate toward yourself. You will need to be creative and responsive in order to develop a stepped approach to inner development, knowing when to be firm, how much work to do when, and when to rest or play.

Animals, like the mind, are sensitive and wonderfully complex beings. If you find it difficult to imagine training a monkey or an elephant, think of a small puppy. At times, you will need to be firm and discipline the little one, but you should never be violent or aggressive. If you are wise, affectionate, and nurturing, the puppy will come to love you and will eagerly respond to the precious time spent together in training.

Meditation can be very easy or very difficult, depending on the handler's temperament. Due to personality, background, and karmic connections, some people are naturally attentive, warm, and generous; others are naturally stiff, anxious, and intense; and some are much too loose and scattered for their own good.

The way we handle our thoughts and emotions has a direct effect on the way we handle others and the world, and how we handle others and the world will have a direct effect on our ability to handle our own mind. They are never separate.

The important thing to remember is that, regardless of our starting point or current situation, we all have access to our innate buddha nature through meditation—through familiarity with the experiences of mindfulness and awareness. We all have the same potential to recognize our difficulties, overcome them, and become enlightened for the benefit of one and all.

9. How to Meditate

Prepare to let go of all thoughts.
Be fully present with the stillness and warmth of heart.
The journey from head to heart is the way of meditation.
The journey to now is the way of meditation.
To move from the stressful ego state of mind
to the peaceful natural state of mind
is the way of meditation.

THIS CHAPTER PROVIDES a basic framework you can use to build your own meditation practice.

PREPARING A SACRED SPACE

Find a peaceful place to practice in. If possible, create a shrine room or a special corner in your living room or bedroom. Create your own altar or use a small table to hold objects that are sacred to you, such as a statue of Buddha, crystals, an image of your spiritual guide, an eagle feather, or any kind of art that is sacred to you.

Even if your meditation space is temporary, prepare it with the same gratitude and reverence. Bring grace and dignity to your every move.

If you have the opportunity, try meditating outside in a natural place of beauty where the air is fresh. Here, there is no need to create a special place. All of nature is sacred. The altar is already set before you.

OFFERINGS

Traditionally in Tibet, part of creating a sacred space is placing five offerings on an altar: a candle, water, incense, fresh flowers, and food, such as fruit, cookies, or candies. These symbolize the most beautiful and enjoyable forms for the eye, smells for the nose, sounds for the ear, tastes for the tongue, and sensations for the body.

Making the five offerings externally helps purify us internally of the five negative emotions: candlelight purifies anger, water purifies ignorance, incense purifies attachment, flowers purify pride, and food purifies envy.

Making offerings trains us in the ways of gratitude, humility, and generosity. It helps shape an attitude or approach to life that results in countless spiritual and physical blessings.

FINDING TIME

Although any available time is good for meditation, try to meditate in the morning. This is when the air is the cleanest, your mind is fresh, your organs and inner channels are empty and clear, and you are least likely to be interrupted.

The length and type of practice you set will evolve over time. To begin with, it is better to have short, fresh meditations than to force yourself into longer sessions. They should be periods of rest and ease that you look forward to.

For the first few weeks, try meditating for about ten or fifteen minutes each morning and, if possible, before you go to bed. When you are ready, gradually extend your formal practice into longer sessions of twenty to forty-five minutes. If you have time, try a mini-retreat, meditating before breakfast, lunch, dinner, and bedtime.

Part of the training and familiarity (*gom*) that supports spiritual growth comes from a regular pattern of practice. Set a pattern that works for you and make a commitment to keep it, for your own well-being. It will soon become an invitation you won't want to miss.

PREPARING YOURSELF

Preparing to meditate should be a relaxing, enjoyable process. Spending some time in any activity (or inactivity) that helps to clear your mind and relax your body will provide a natural opening into a more formal meditation session.

You may want to dim the lights, play some meditational music, take some time to read and reflect on spiritual writings, or write in a special journal reserved for personal or spiritual reflection.

COMFORT

Make sure you are as relaxed as possible; wear loose-fitting or stretchy clothing. Have a comfortable cushion or mattress to sit on. You may need a meditation belt for extra support, or a straight-backed chair if you are unable to sit cross-legged on the floor.

Remove any metal objects you may be wearing, such as watches, rings, earrings, or other jewelry. These items may interfere with the subtle flow of *lung* energy.

PURIFICATION

After acknowledging the sacred space where you will meditate, it is time to acknowledge your own sacred essence and pay attention to anything that may be obscuring it.

This is a process of renewal and purification. It includes consciously selecting and then letting go of specific mental and emotional disturbances, making way for a return to inner harmony and energetic balance.

There are many purification rituals that can be done before entering the main part of a meditation session. A few of the most common of these include the following:

- ▸ Prostrations.
- ▸ Breathing practices, such as the nine-breath purification (chapter 14).
- ▸ Yoga-like movements, such as the *tsa lung* exercises (chapter 16).

At times, you may choose to do one of these for the entire session, in which case it would serve as the main practice itself.

Although it is not essential, the act of washing yourself can serve as a symbolic connection to your own inner purification. If you can't take a shower or bath, at least wash your hands and face and brush your teeth. Such cleansing rituals leave you feeling fresh and clean and can have a positive effect on your mood and your mindset as you prepare to meditate.

FIVE-POINT POSTURE

Begin your meditation session by sitting comfortably, preferably in what is called the five-point posture:

1. If possible, sit down in the cross-legged lotus position.
2. Straighten your spine while lifting and opening your chest.
3. Slightly bend your neck.
4. Relax your eyes and, with your eyelids almost but not quite shut, gaze down and out into the space about a foot beyond your nose. For beginners, if this is too distracting, the eyes can be fully closed.
5. Rest your hands comfortably, either on your knees or just below the navel in the classic position of equipoise. There are a number of ways to do this. Traditionally, Bönpos place the tip of their thumb at the base of their ring finger on each hand and then place the upturned left hand on top of the upturned right hand that is resting on the lap.

The most important point is to keep your spine as relaxed and straight as possible within a comfortable position that you'll be able to maintain without fidgeting or moving too much. This might be sitting cross-legged on the floor, sitting up in a chair, or lying on your back.

Straightening the spine straightens and opens physical and energetic channels, allowing for the unobstructed flow of breath, blood, and *lung*. This helps calm the body and keep the mind clear and alert.

The cross-legged posture is the most stable, self-supporting, and effortless position to sit in. It supports a straight spine from a broad, four-cornered base that widely distributes body weight and has the added advantage of holding in the body's core heat, keeping the legs and feet warm—extremely important features where I come from.

Unfortunately, many people cannot sit comfortably in this position. If you are one of them, don't worry. Comfort is critical, so find a position that will hold you and your spine in the straightest and most comfortable way.

THE BASIC MEDITATION SEQUENCE

All meditation sessions have a beginning, a middle, and an end. They start with an intention, move into the middle or main practice, and close with a dedication.

INTENTION

The mind of great compassion always carries the yearning to attain enlightenment in order to help others do the same. Any meditative practice should always begin with this intention.

Often, our intention is very limited, which leads to limited results. For example, if we intend to reduce our stress through meditation, we may never get beyond the limiting experience of temporary stress relief for ourselves alone.

If we set our sights higher and seek to relieve all suffering for all beings, then the result of our spiritual practice is likely to be much greater and stronger.

The following is a beautiful expression of intention that is a favorite of His Holiness the Fourteenth Dalai Lama. The first two verses come from Shakyashribhadra's *Seven-Limb Entryway into the Practice of the True Dharma*, and the last is from Shantideva's *Guide to the Bodhisattva's Way of Life*.

> With a wish to free all beings
> I shall always go for refuge
> To the Buddha, Dharma, and Sangha,
> Until I reach full enlightenment.
>
> Enthused by wisdom and compassion,
> Today in the Buddha's presence
> I generate the Mind for Full Awakening
> For the benefit of all sentient beings.
>
> As long as space remains,
> As long as sentient beings remain,
> Until then, may I too remain,
> And dispel the miseries of the world.

MAIN PRACTICE

The main practice you select for a session will depend on your current circumstances and level of spiritual training. Regardless, all sessions can begin by spending at least a few minutes in simple breathing awareness to settle body and mind. Then you may go on to a deeper level of spiritual practice including, for example, the following:

- ▸ Calm-abiding meditation (chapter 10).
- ▸ Insight meditation (chapter 11).
- ▸ The nine-breath purification practice (chapter 14).
- ▸ Physical exercises such as *tsa lung* (chapter 16).
- ▸ Mantra chanting (chapter 20).

DEDICATION

Just as a meditation session begins with setting the intention to benefit yourself and others, it closes by dedicating or extending any merit you have received from the practice to your family, your community, and all beings.

The dedication prayer could be your own simple and heartfelt words, such as:

I dedicate this practice to all beings:
May we all be free from suffering and the causes of suffering;
May we all dwell in peace and harmony.

Here is the English version of the Tibetan prayer of dedication from the Bön tradition:

All pure virtue done through the
    three doors,
I dedicate to the welfare of all sentient beings of the
    three realms.
After having purified all obstacles and obscurations of the
    three times,
May we swiftly achieve the complete buddhahood of the
    three bodies.[8]

INTEGRATION

When you have completed your meditation, sit quietly for a short time to gather your thoughts and feelings from the session. Be aware of what you may have discovered within the stillness, silence, and clarity of your meditation. Now generate determination to carry this energy into your everyday life.

10. Calm-Abiding Meditation

During breathing meditation, I hear the breath in my heart.
I am aware of breathing in and out.
The sound of breathing through my nostrils is balanced.
Breathing goes to a deeper level, no longer shallow.
My body and mind are unified.
I am peaceful because my breath has become balanced.

THERE ARE REALLY only two kinds of meditation, which together give rise to the thousands of different meditation methods and practices from cultures and religions around the world. One is calm-abiding meditation, called *shamatha* in Sanskrit and *zhiné* in Tibetan. The second is insight meditation, called *vipashyana* in Sanskrit and *lhagthong* in Tibetan.

ZHINÉ, OR CALM-ABIDING MEDITATION

Calm-abiding meditation exercises are mainly methods that use mindfulness to calm and settle the mind. *Zhi* means "calm" or "peace," and *né* means "abide," "remain," or "stay with"; zhiné is the practice of remaining in a calm, clear state of mind.

Entering a state of calm-abiding is entering a state of single-pointed concentration and mental stability. This can only happen when the mind is no longer scattered or wandering and is free from distraction, excitation, and dullness.

As the mind settles, negative emotions will spontaneously diminish and wisdom-awareness will arise, along with more joy and peace. This process is like a glass of dirty water becoming clear again as the dirt settles.

During zhiné meditation, an attribute or focus of attention is used. It could be any number of things such as a candle flame, a visualization, a statue, or a sound. In some traditions, zhiné training includes using the Tibetan letter ཨ (AH) as a visual object of focus.

However, one of the most effective and convenient attributes used by practitioners around the world is the breath as it enters and leaves the body. The practitioner fully inhabits the present by placing the mind, moment-by-moment, on the rhythm and sensations of the breath.

It is important to develop and stabilize mindfulness of breathing and the experience of calm-abiding by first practicing in silence and solitude in a peaceful place. Once you're familiar with zhiné, it can then be done anywhere, anytime. Try it at the doctor's office, in a traffic jam, or on the phone while waiting on hold. Zhiné will always make the mind more open, calm, and ready to achieve whatever goal has been set and to respond skillfully to whatever situation presents itself.

I practice zhiné on the golf course and find that as soon as I breathe with mindfulness, there is an immediate effect; my golf game improves significantly. I breathe in and out two or three times and remind myself to relax and be still.

I remember golfing a few years ago with three other men at a beautiful golf course on Vancouver Island. I was tired, frustrated, and playing poorly. We arrived at the twelfth hole and the others started to tee off. I stepped back, sat down cross-legged on the grass, closed my eyes, and began to meditate. I focused on calming my breath and letting go of my thoughts and frustrations.

The three men stared at me with no idea of what I was doing. They maybe even thought I was a little crazy. After a few minutes, I stood up and started to play again.

Everything had changed. I was calm and peaceful, my swing was good, and the rest of my game was wonderful. This experience was real encouragement for me to stop and take time for mindfulness, especially when things are not going well.

ZHINÉ EXERCISES

The following are a number of breathing exercises that can be used to cultivate calm-abiding. All of them use breath as the attribute, or focus, of meditation and are done by breathing in through the nostrils and out through the mouth. The first exercise below, "In Through the Nose, Out Through the Mouth," is the basis for the subsequent exercises.

Remember to relax. Let your inhalation and exhalation be slow and deep. Also, pause for a second to two at the end of each one instead of switching right away from one to the other.

IN THROUGH THE NOSE, OUT THROUGH THE MOUTH

- ► Breathe in slowly and deeply through the nostrils. Listen to the air as it is pulled in. Feel your diaphragm, lungs, and stomach expand.
- ► Now exhale through the mouth with an audible *whoooo*, releasing any tension or stress.
- ► Repeat this as many times as you wish.

COUNTING THE BREATH

A. *From One to Five*

- ► As you breathe in, mentally count from one to five.
- ► As you breathe out, mentally count from one to seven.
- ► Repeat as many times as you wish. Notice the difference it makes in settling the body and mind.

B. From One to Eight

- As you breathe in, mentally count from one to eight.
- As you breathe out, mentally count from one to eight.
- Repeat as many times as you wish.
- Notice the difference it makes in settling the body and mind.

This longer, balanced count helps clear and open the sinuses.

C. From One to Twenty-Five

- Inhale and exhale fully for one count.
- Count up to twenty-five while breathing in this way.
- If you lose count, start over.
- Try doing three sets of counting up to twenty-five.

These counting methods are a good way to learn and to check how aware and focused you are. They are also very helpful in settling the mind when it is disturbed or distracted. Eventually, however, counting will no longer be necessary. The mind and awareness of breathing will become one. This perfect balance is the state of calm-abiding.

BREATHING WITH HEAD MOVEMENT

- As you breathe in, lift the chin and arch the neck, tipping the head back.
- As you breathe out, lower the chin and curl the neck, dropping the head forward.
- Repeat as many times as you wish.

BREATHING WITH THOUGHTS

- As you breathe in, mentally say to yourself, "I'm breathing in."
- As you breathe out, say, "I know I'm breathing out."

Or

- As you breathe in, say, "I'm resting."
- As you breathe out, say, "I feel peace."

You can choose your own words to say: for example, *I feel free, strong, peaceful, safe, quiet, etc.* Be sure they are words that help you to feel peaceful.

BREATHING WITH VISUALIZATION

- As you breathe in through the nostrils, visualize a white light filling your whole body. Feel luminous, like a buddha. Feel the light of compassion.
- As you breathe out, visualize your breath as white light of compassion and send this kindness to others.
- Repeat as many times as you wish.

Take some time to try each of the exercises described in this section and select the ones that you connect with and find most effective. Whichever ones you use, remember that when you connect to the breath, you are connecting to your true nature and the source of bliss and joy within.

11. Insight Meditation

Sit quietly doing nothing.
Leave everything as it is, without judgment.
As thoughts arise, let them come.
As thoughts leave, let them go.
Don't chase them.
Don't stop them.
Leave them as they are.
Remain in the natural state.

LHAGTHONG is the Tibetan word for insight meditation. It is translated into English as "superior seeing," "great vision," or "supreme wisdom." The term *lhag* means "higher," "superior," or "greater," and *thong* means "seeing" or "knowing."

When you look through your eyes, you can see that an object has color, shape, and size. However, the true nature of that object is more than that. Lhagthong is seeing beyond what appears to the ordinary mind to apprehend the fullness, wholeness, and entirety of any and all phenomena. It is seeing and knowing that emptiness is the foundation of everything; that nothing exists independently, from its own side. This is the ultimate view of insight meditation, where seeing means knowing, knowing means realizing, and realizing means experiencing the nature of reality, beyond appearances.

Insight meditation exercises mainly use *shezin*, which is the sense of awareness itself, as the focus. Aware of what? Aware of itself. Aware of everything—thinking, feeling, seeing, hearing, tasting, smelling, touching; aware of impermanence and death. Aware that without death there is no life and without life there is no death.

Insight meditation brings our awareness into the present moment. In that moment, if we are fully aware of something, our consciousness becomes unified with that object.

For example, when you look at a flower in the normal, dualistic way you will see that it is different from your mind and vice versa. But when you fully enter the present moment with no thought of the past or future, you are fully present with the flower, beyond dualistic thinking. You are being with the flower one hundred percent. This unification of mind and object is the state of insight meditation.

UNION OF ZHINÉ AND LHAGTHONG

During zhiné meditation, the mind calms down as disturbing thoughts and emotions settle. That settling provides the clarity needed for insight. As I was taught:

> *Jezhi, Jezhi, nonmong zhi,*
> *Jesal, Jesal, yeshe sal.*
> The calmer and calmer the affliction (or emotion),
> The clearer and clearer the wisdom (or awareness).

According to the Tibetan Bön tradition, calm-abiding meditation is taught and practiced first. Once the stability of zhiné becomes familiar, insight meditation is then added and the two become one. This union, called *zhilhak sungdrel* in Tibetan, is extremely important for spiritual transformation.

Zhiné is like the foundation and walls of a house. Lhagthong is like candlelight inside the house. Without a house, the flame may be easily disturbed or destroyed by wind. A good house with a solid foundation guarantees a safe place for the light.

Both zhiné and lhagthong are antidotes for afflictions and for the wild and slothful habits of mind. Although zhiné purifies and liberates one from gross mental and emotional obstacles, it does not get to the root of those afflictions. It's like picking up all the trash, clothes, and dirty dishes around the house before a deeper cleaning can be done.

There is a story of a Hindu yogi who practiced only calm-abiding meditation for many years. He did not eat, move, talk, or take a break of any kind during all of those years. One day he came out of his meditation. He saw that his hair and beard had grown very long and lay all around him. "Oh, I've been in meditation for a very long time," he said. He was amazed and very proud of his accomplishment. But as he stood up, he became aware of an ugly mess in his hair. A mouse had made a nest there.

The yogi immediately became upset, releasing the three poisons: anger at the mouse, attachment to his hair, and ignorance of the true condition of his mind and the root of his afflictions.

Even though he had been in meditation for such a long time, his practice was incomplete. Without insight, he remained in darkness. He still had not cleared the seeds of anger, pride, and ego-attachment.

Zhiné itself will not liberate you. The darkness of mental and emotional afflictions can only be dispelled by the light of wisdom that comes from the union of calm-abiding and insight meditation.

TWO KINDS OF LHAGTHONG

There are two types of insight meditation. Both represent a state of mind that has reached a superior or higher level of clarity and awareness. Both are beyond the ordinary thinking mind.

The first kind of lhagthong is called *jok gom*. It is an abiding meditation that uses the ultimate truth as the object. The practitioner sees the nature of everything as emptiness and abides in that infinite space of mind. It's as though the eyes are closed with nothing seen but the infinite, empty space of the natural state of mind. In *jok gom*, one simply remains in that state.

The other kind of insight meditation is called *ché gom*. It is an investigation meditation that uses the relative truth as the object. It is the awareness of appearances as relative, temporary, and empty of their own separate, inherent existence. Ché gom is recognizing that emptiness is form and form is emptiness. It's as though the eyes are wide open, clearly seeing everything, all around.

For example, in ché gom, the details of the cup I'm holding are seen—the top, the handle, the bottom, the design painted on the side—and questions might arise, "What is it made of? Who made it? Where did it come from?"

The questions are part of a method that leads to the experience of insight and clarity itself. They are made while remaining fully present, in a nondualistic way, with the subject. However, once the actual state of ché gom is reached, there are no questions, only answers. There's nothing to find. Just as we leave counting behind to fully enter into zhiné, we eventually leave questioning behind to fully enter and remain in the mental state of clear awareness that is lhagthong.

INSIGHT MEDITATION EXERCISES

As with zhiné, there are many methods for cultivating the awareness of lhagthong. One of the most important of these is simply observing your own thoughts and emotions while you are meditating. The following visualization will help you do that.

WATCHING YOUR THOUGHTS

Imagine yourself sitting in the middle of a large room with many windows and doors in all four walls. Get up and open all the doors and windows and return to your seat. Your responsibility is to remain in the middle, on your chair. Your chair has wheels on the legs so you are able to turn around in a circle.

All kinds of people, forms, thoughts, ideas, memories, and experiences will enter and exit through the doors and windows. They come and go from different directions through different openings. You simply watch. Who is coming? Who is leaving? Just watch. Don't chase after or follow. Don't invite or reject. Don't pull in or push away. Just watch. If someone goes, be aware they are going. If someone comes, be aware they have entered. No judging, rejecting, or chasing. Watch! Observe!

I clearly remember doing this as a child when we were visiting the city of Chengdu in China. I had my face pressed to the window of the hotel room, looking down onto the bustling street. There were so many different people, with unique ways of talking, dressing, and moving. Time slipped away as I simply enjoyed the watching. I felt like a cat, alert and fascinated, watching birds fluttering around outside.

Similarly, in this practice, just relax and look at all the thoughts and emotions coming and going. Just watch.

Usually, if we like something, we reach or grasp for it, or run after it. If we don't like something, we try rejecting it, or fighting it, or pushing it away. Either way, we are in a pulling or pushing struggle. In this meditation, just observe. Watch. Be aware.

The doors and windows are your six senses: seeing, hearing, smelling, tasting, feeling (touching), and thinking. All of the doors are open. Be willing to leave them open and allow what comes and goes to just "be."

Don't fight any of the sounds, thoughts, forms, or feelings. Be a bright, clear, nonjudging, impartial observer of all that comes and goes within that room of your mind.

If you can remain on your seat with openness and trust, fear and ego will transform into compassion and your visiting thoughts will transform into awareness. What you have to gain from this meditation is insight, the gift that opens up choices and possibilities.

SEARCHING FOR ME

For this insight meditation, spend some time searching for who you really are. Seek your true nature from the top of your head to the bottom of your feet and back again. Repeat this kind of scan over and over, observing and searching for your authentic self.

Who are you? Where is the "I" of your identity? Where is your mind? Is there any color, shape, size, edge, or center of your mind? You may or may not find anything, but keep searching. No one else can do this work for you.

Eventually, you will come to a clear realization that there is really nothing to be found. However, finding nothing is not nothingness. Emptiness is not nothingness. To realize that phenomena are empty of what they appear to be at first—individual and separate—is to realize the fullness and infinite potential of all things. This opens the door to a direct experience of the true nature of mind.

Without insight, we tend to assume that the basis of our identity is our body and our ordinary mind. Trying to imagine anything beyond that might feel threatening or even devastating.

However, to experience emptiness is to experience the fullness of reality and the highest state of bliss. I can only suggest or point to these things briefly here. A deeper understanding requires the direct experiences of zhiné and insight meditation and the instruction of a qualified teacher.

SKY GAZING

Another traditional insight meditation practice is sky gazing, which must be done on a clear day. Lie down on your back, facing up to a clear blue sky. Relax and just stare into the sky. At first, you connect with it externally, but as you stare in complete relaxation, you will end up connecting internally as well. When this happens, you experience and connect to what Tibetans call *namkha sumjor*, the union of three spaces: the external sky space, the internal eye space, and the innermost space of the mind. The discovery of that union is the discovery of your true nature.

DZOGCHEN

As described in the section on calm-abiding meditation, an attribute is something to focus on, like a candle, certain thoughts, an image, or the breath.

Meditation with no attribute means meditation with no object of focus. It is a direct connection to emptiness that is the nondual, non-discursive, natural state of the mind. It is mind looking directly at itself. That state is rigpa, primordial awareness, buddha nature, or nature of mind. This is the view of Dzogchen, the Great Perfection teaching.

Although the breath is no longer a focus in Dzogchen practice, it is still operating automatically in the background. It is the vehicle that carries the mind all the way through from birth to death and from zhiné to lhagthong to the realization of Dzogchen.

Dzogchen is the highest meditational philosophy, according to the Nyingma and Bön traditions of Tibet. The word *dzogchen* means "great perfection." It is great because when you follow instruction and experience your true nature of mind, you experience great bliss, great fulfillment, and all the great qualities that spontaneously arise from wisdom and compassion.

It is perfect because when you experience your true nature, you wake up from all the pain and pleasure of the delusional, ordinary mind and realize the primordially perfect essence of all things. This is a state beyond words. It is a state beyond karmic conditions; there is no good/bad, he/she, friend/enemy. Everything is primordially perfect, as it is.

Dzogchen practice may start with effort, but it reaches beyond effort. It may start with an object but reaches beyond object. What we call Dzogchen meditation is really no meditation. As with emptiness, it's not easy to understand with the ordinary mind. It is discovered by resting in the natural state of mind, which is the primordial awareness that is beyond the ordinary mind.

The following is a simple but profound poem written by the great master Dawa Gyaltsen, which summarizes the Dzogchen view:

THE FIVE-FOLD TEACHING OF DAWA GYALTSEN

> Vision is mind.
> Mind is emptiness.
> Emptiness is clear light.
> Clear light is union.
> Union is great bliss.

Although the poem looks simple, fully understanding it requires explanations and instructions from a Dzogchen teacher.

LEAVE EVERYTHING AS IT IS

For Dzogchen practice, you simply sit quietly doing nothing. Leave everything as it is without judgment. As thoughts arise, let them arise; as thoughts leave, let them go. Don't chase them. Don't stop them. Leave them as they are and remain in the natural state.

All thoughts and emotions arise from, remain in, and dissolve back into the empty space of mind. When you recognize and experience that, you are practicing Dzogchen meditation. The instruction is to remain and abide in that space, that natural state of mind.

This practice can be very easy or very difficult depending on your personality, your level of instruction, the quality of your practice, and your karmic connection to the Dzogchen view.

One of the most important points I learned from Dzogchen teachings is to remain natural, without fabrication, and leave whatever is happening as it is—not trying to fix, force, or correct anything—simply letting go and letting be.

12. It Makes a Difference

My sacred body,
my pure mind,
resting together in the rhythm of breath,
their every need cared for by mindfulness and awareness;
an indivisible team,
an indescribable joy.

MEDITATION GENERATES a vast array of physical, mental, and spiritual benefits that have been experienced in my culture for thousands of years. Many of these effects have now been understood and verified in Western cultures through scientific research.

Following are some of the main ways meditation makes a real difference to the health and well-being of practitioners.

CONNECTION

By bringing simple attention to the natural rhythm of our breath, we connect body and mind, inside and outside, physical and spiritual.

Breathing in and out is a great exchange, taking place on many levels. Most obviously, it is the exchange of stale, used air and carbon dioxide for fresh, life-giving air full of oxygen. In meditation, this cycle of taking in what we need and letting go of what we don't becomes a pattern for maintaining physical and mental health.

As the breath settles, so does the mind. This, in turn, calms the central nervous system, improves the heart–brain connection, and strengthens nerve connections in key areas of the brain. A number of nerve-connection chemicals involved in our sense of happiness increase during meditation.[9]

Mindfulness of breathing can act as a bridge, connecting us fully to whatever situation we are in. If I want to speak to you, for example, I connect to my breathing first and then proceed to connect to you with a "calm breath, calm mind." Using my breath as a bridge in this way improves my mental balance and my performance, regardless of what I'm doing.

Being disconnected from our true nature causes energetic imbalances and blockages that result in dissatisfaction and dis-ease. Regular meditation reconnects us to a sense of ease and satisfaction. It is a tool anyone can use to generate positive energy and well-being. These things are not found somewhere outside, but within you—right here, right now. They are part of the natural state of mind that you can connect to at any time by becoming awake and aware.

CONCENTRATION

Through meditation, we train the mind to relax, focus, and eventually stay focused for extended periods of time. Being able to do this is beneficial not only in meditation but in anything we choose to do.

Meditative concentration increases our ability to listen, learn, remember, make decisions, solve problems, set intentions, and follow through with effective action. It heightens the clarity and vividness of sensory perception.

Mindful breathing improves physical and mental performance in all aspects of daily living, including, for example, athletic competition, university exams, pain management, coping with conflict, and improving memory.

When I'm golfing, I use a breathing technique to help me relax my muscles, focus my mind, and control my swing. As I bring the club up, I breathe in slowly through my nostrils. As I swing, I push the air out forcefully through my nostrils.

This kind of mindful breathing sharpens my concentration while stopping all other thoughts and emotions. Once I became familiar with the method, it was like magic for my golf game.

REGULATION

In the silence of meditation, the mind becomes more settled and balanced, which directly influences the balance and regulation of bodily systems, including air flow, blood flow, water balance, muscle tension, temperature, weight, hormone levels, and brain activity.

One of the most important benefits of mindfulness meditation is the ability it gives us to notice negative thoughts and emotions and see how they obstruct our well-being and how they can be transformed by their antidotes.

Love transforms anger; generosity transforms greed and desire; knowledge and wisdom transform ignorance and confusion; openness transforms envy and jealousy; peace transforms pride and arrogance; diligence transforms indolence and sloth.

Meditation helps us harmonize not only the net of interactions within our own body and mind but also our net of interactions within our family, our society, and the entire universe.

In meditation, we discover that we are not separate from others or our world. Through that experience, we naturally develop spontaneous love and compassion for others. We become more understanding and less judgmental. We become more accepting, patient, and tolerant.

Oddly, as we become more open and other-focused in our practice, we develop more self-acceptance, self-control, self-determination, and self-confidence.

RESTORATION

Taking time to meditate is like taking time to restore your battery. It is literally rejuvenating for body, mind, and spirit.

Meditation has been shown to reduce inflammation, improve pain management, and strengthen immunity. The result is not only less illness but more resilience and better recovery in the face of illness and injury.

Mindfulness and awareness practices are becoming increasingly popular prescriptions for addressing the anxiety- and stress-related disorders that plague modern society. They have been shown to increase levels of key chemicals that sustain tissues and organs; reduce stress; enhance pleasure; strengthen the immune system; alleviate physical pain and pain associated with depression, stress, and anxiety; and help regulate sleep and waking cycles.[10]

GESHELA IN GAMMA

A few years ago, my good friend Dr. Tom Diamond invited me to participate in some neurofeedback and brain-mapping research. Tom is a doctor of psychology who specializes in neurotechnology and brain health.

The process involved wearing a cap of tiny electrodes that sent electrical information from the brain to an electroencephalograph (EEG) machine that translated the information into colorful maps of brain functioning.

I very quickly learned how revealing the EEG is. My thoughts and feelings were literally exposed on an open screen. I remember thinking there was nowhere for me to hide or pretend.

Tom scanned my brain while I was just sitting there, and then again while I was meditating. Afterward, he told me he was amazed at the brain wave changes he saw while I was meditating and gave a quick explanation:

There are five different types of brain waves, with different frequencies (measured in hertz) that are produced according to your mood and activity:

Wave	Hertz	Description	Experience
delta	1–3	very slow; brain is "turned off"	deepest stages of sleep
theta	4–8	slow but conscious	dream-like "third-eye" state (seeing in a different visionary way, beyond the normal optical perception of the eyes)
alpha	8–12	faster, alert, relaxed; happy waves	good mood; calm but awake
beta	13–35	fast, focused; "work-horse waves"	thinking, planning, problem-solving
gamma	40–80	fastest wave	experience is not fast but spacious, slow, or timeless

Although all five waves are always present to some degree in the brain, the meditator is able to change their volumes and their experience.

Beginner meditators are soon able to slow their brain down, shifting out of the common, high-performance beta waves into slower, more pleasant and relaxed waves. They learn how to turn up the volume of some frequencies and turn down others.

After thousands of hours of practice, an experienced meditator is able to turn up the special high-frequency gamma wave and turn everything else off. This is a kind of leap frog over the slower waves into the high speed but profoundly calm and healing gamma state of mind. Witnessing such a shift in my brain is what amazed Tom. "This," he said, "is Geshela in gamma."

When I'm in that state it feels like I could stay there forever, like I never want to be separate from it. My mind becomes clearer and more aware of everything. My body feels different, like I am floating.

Things change inside of me. For example, my perception becomes more positive and less influenced by stress and worry. I have a sense of unity, of being fully connected to myself and everything around me at the same time. I feel joyful, blissful, content, and completely silent in body and mind.

When I'm ready to go out into the world again, I try to bring the calm, still presence of my meditation experience with me. It is like medicine that protects me and makes me more effective in everything I do and with everyone I meet. Carrying meditative awareness into my day makes it easier to notice and face challenges as they arise and to deal with them to the best of my ability.

LIMITLESS POTENTIAL

The history of the meditation practices I have learned reaches back to the early years of Tibet, when many spiritual masters went into caves in the high mountains to spend a number of years or even a lifetime in meditation. As there was no easy access to medicine or medical practitioners, they had to rely on their own resources to manage their health.

These masters developed and eventually taught special practices known as *keksel* to protect practitioners from any kind of sickness during their spiritual journey. *Kek* means "obstacle" and *sel* means "purification." In this case, the obstacle refers to physical or mental affliction that is purified through exercises that combine breathing, meditation, and physical movement.

Keksel provides practitioners temporary benefits by helping to protect their health and overcome disease. It also provides ultimate benefits by generating inner bliss and happiness and providing a gateway to higher levels of realization, all the way to perfect enlightenment.

The physical benefits of keksel are a support for the ultimate benefits of meditation itself. Advanced practitioners are able to generate their own heat and survive with very little to eat or drink. Their meditation actually becomes their clothing and their food. We have a

Tibetan saying that recognizes this accomplishment: *"Ting nge zin kö, ting nge zin zay,"* where *ting nge zin* means "meditation" or "concentration," *kö* means "clothes," and *zay* means "food." So: "Meditation as clothes; meditation as food."

A modern example of such an advanced practitioner is the Tibetan Bön master Namkha Gyaltsen, who passed away in 2020. He spent over twenty years in solitary retreat in the sacred Kongpo region of central Tibet. He was nicknamed the *"shuk tok* lama" because he survived almost solely on his daily food of *shuk tok*, the pea-sized cones of the cedar tree in his area.

You might find such feats unbelievable, but we have another saying for that: "Just because you haven't seen it doesn't mean it doesn't exist." The accomplishments of Olympic athletes are also shocking: the extreme speed of a sprinter, the amazing strength and flexibility of a gymnast, and the awesome feats of a rock climber.

All of these things point to the possibility and power of meditative concentration. With practice and training, our capacity and realization will expand beyond what we presently consider to be "normal." The amazing potential of meditation is not confined to others or to the past. It is open to us right now.

Regardless of where we are in our spiritual development, meditation always makes a difference. It is the way to liberate ourselves from ego and become free of the ignorance and confusion that lie at the root of all suffering. It is the way to happiness for ourselves and all beings. It is the way to realize the limitless potential of loving-kindness, compassion, joy, and equanimity.

PART IV

Breath and Visualization

13. Seeing in a Different Way

For the first time,
I see the different colors
of the breath within me,
and they are stunning in their natural beauty.
I cannot turn away.

VISUALIZATION IS SEEING in a different way. It's a creative process of using the imagination to produce a full mental image of something, not just a visual one.

For example, if I think of holding a little puppy, I might or might not see a clear visual image, but I also sense things like its soft, furry body in my arms, the smell of its puppy breath, and the way it squirms and leaps up to lick my face. Although all of this is fabricated and dream-like, it will actually flood my body and mind with all of the positive energy and biochemical responses that real joy, laughter, and intense love bring.

Thinking and visualizing go together. When you think of someone you love, you "see" them in your mind. You feel their presence and warm connection to you. Whether you notice or not, you and your visualization have become one.

On the other hand, if you bring to mind someone you don't like or someone who has hurt you, you'll "see" them in your mind's eye as a complex of appearances, thoughts, and emotions such as resentment or anger. Those feelings can change your mood and energetic make-up. The unhappiness, anxiety, or disappointment associated with that person may actually show up on your face or in your pounding heart. If such negative thoughts and projections persist, they will affect everything in and around you, including your mind, body, health, work, and relationships.

The good news here is that our ability to visualize can be used to help us shift out of negative habitual tendencies and become happier, healthier, and kinder human beings.

COMMON VISUALIZATION PRACTICES

TRANSFORMING SUFFERING

Tonglen practice develops the courage of compassion through the power of visualization. One brings to mind another person, "sees" their suffering, and imagines taking it into one's own heart on the in-breath. There it is transformed into whatever is needed or useful for the other and is sent back to them, carried on the out-breath. Tonglen as a healing practice is described in detail in chapter 7.

BREATHING LIGHT

Another powerful combination of breathing and visualization practice is to imagine inhaling pure white light through the nostrils with every breath. The light goes everywhere in the body, purifying any physical, mental, or emotional struggles. Exhale through the nostrils and, with every out-breath, imagine releasing all negativities into the ground. Mother earth receives and transforms them, leaving your body and mind relaxed and in a blissful, luminous state.

A similar practice was taught to me by my very close Cree friend and spiritual brother, Alex Ahenakew. It is used in preparation for receiving a vision. As above, you completely fill your body with peaceful, healing white light and then just rest, breathing deeply and slowly. When it is ready, a vision will appear naturally.

The simple healing exercises described in chapter 6 are a variation of the "breathing light" visualization that can be used to manage pain. The first step is to identify which emotion, stressor, or physical pain is the problem. What exactly is causing the pain? Where is it? When did it start?

Once the pain has been acknowledged, using your imagination, breathe pure, white, healing light down into your belly. Now, while holding the breath, send the light to wherever the pain is. As you continue to hold your breath and your pain in the presence of this light, the pain begins to dissolve. Release it with the breath in the form of black smoke that dissolves into the ground.

Repeat this exercise as much as is needed. You may not notice any change at first. This kind of exercise takes some practice to be effective, but it will, eventually, result in a beneficial energetic release.

IMAGINING PERFECTION

Close your eyes and imagine the most beautiful, peaceful place you can. It's the perfect place to relax and meditate. Imagine that all the people around you there are beautiful, kind, and peaceful. There is no need to pretend, defend, or be on guard with them in any way. They are totally loving and caring.

Now imagine that your own body is also beautiful, perfect, and luminous. Instead of being critical, picky, or fussy about any aspect of it, you are completely content and grateful for this wonderful body.

Everything is pure and perfect: the place, the people, and yourself. This kind of visualization can inspire and transform you.

IMAGINING ENLIGHTENMENT

An ordinary practitioner can transform by merging with the imagined form, qualities, and symbols of an extraordinary, enlightened being. This concept is at the heart of tantric practice and is one of the highest and best uses of visualization.

By repeatedly producing an image representing the enlightened qualities we yearn for and connecting to it with all of the senses, we can eventually become what we've imagined.

Tantric practice is a combination of breathing awareness, mantra recitation, and detailed visualizations of enlightened beings and their mandalas. Its purpose is transformation: negative emotion transforms into wisdom, the ordinary body transforms into a luminous body, pain transforms into pleasure, and suffering transforms into happiness.

14. The Nine-Breath Purification Practice

Channels of white, red, and blue are the path.
Breath is the vehicle.
Awareness is the driver.
Together, they will take us where we want to be.

IN THIS CHAPTER we will explore in detail how to generate and enter the creative, transformative world of visualization through a special meditation called *lungro gutruk*, the nine-breath purification. It is a combination of breathing and visualizing techniques used to clear and open the unseen energy channels within the body. This is a profound practice treasured by all of the Tibetan spiritual traditions.

The exercise consists of nine complete breaths divided into three sets of three breaths: one set for clearing each of the three main energy channels.

These three channels we discussed in chapter 2 are the pillars of our energetic make-up. They are like a temple within, housing the vibrant, luminous essence of our true nature. For us to function well and flourish, these channels need to be clear of the static and obstruction caused by the three root poisons: aversion, attachment, and ignorance.

It's important to contemplate each one of the poisons and become an expert in how they play out in your own life. Attachment might be showing up in your relationship to loved ones or material things, or as an addiction to your work or a substance. Aversion might show itself in your impatience, frustration, irritability, or avoidance behavior. Ignorance of your true nature might manifest as fear, confusion, anxiety, or selfish behavior.

Main Channel	Color	Root Poison to Clear
right (*kyangma*)	white	aversion (*zhedang*): anger, hatred, pushing away
left (*roma*)	red	attachment (*döchak*): greed, desire, holding
center (*üma*)	dark blue	ignorance (*marigpa*): confusion, not realizing one's true nature

Just as water is used to clean the body, the nine-breath meditation is a cleansing process to purify and wash away our mental and emotional afflictions. For example, if you went for months without showering, you would feel uncomfortable, dirty, and heavy. Similar feelings of discomfort develop at an energetic level without regular cleansing of our psychic and emotional "inner" mind and body. The nine-breath purification is an excellent method for doing just that. As a regular practice, it will keep your mind clean, fresh, alert, and balanced.

HOW TO DO THE NINE-BREATH MEDITATION

How to Breathe

Each of the nine breaths includes a full inhalation and exhalation. Each inhalation is taken in slowly, gently, and deeply. Although your breath is physically being pulled into your lungs, imagine that it is being pulled down into and filling your belly. It carries the clear light of awareness and healing *lung* energy.

There is a special way to exhale that we will call the "nine-breath release," described below. It is a powerful and purifying release of stale air along with energetic disturbances, obstacles, and blockages.

THE NINE-BREATH RELEASE

The nine-breath release is an exhalation that begins as a normal release of air but picks up speed and strength until, at the end, it is forcefully directed, as if thrown toward the ground.

Your belly muscles should contract slightly to help push out the air that is exiting through one or both nostrils with an audible rush. The increasing sound is similar to the sound of an approaching train that seems to pick up speed and volume until it blasts past you and is gone.

VISUALIZE THE THREE CHANNELS

Sit comfortably in the five-point meditation posture. Visualize your central energy channel. It is a deep-blue column, about the diameter of a thick fountain pen. It begins in the center of your abdomen, four finger-widths below the navel, and rises straight up through your core, just in front of the spine. It widens slightly from your heart to its opening at your crown. Imagine the top is wide and open, like a flower.

Now visualize the two side channels. Each one is the thickness of a pencil and joins the central channel at its base below the navel. They rise straight up through the body on either side of the central channel, follow the curve under the skull, pass down just behind the eyes, and open at the nostrils. The right channel is white and the left channel is red.

Remember, these are subtle energy channels within the body, not physical vessels like arteries or veins. They are pathways of energy that can be influenced by directing intention through visualization and the breath.

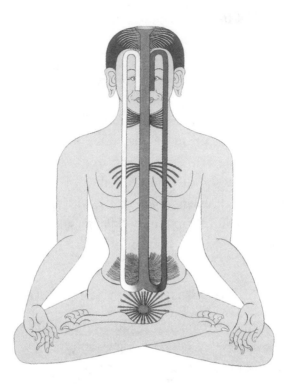

The First Set of Three Breaths

Raise your right hand with the thumb pressing against the middle of the ring finger.[11]

Now close your right nostril with the tip of that right ring finger. Inhale slowly and deeply through your left nostril. Imagine you are breathing in pure green light.[12]

Imagine the air rising up the nostril, passing behind the left eye, then following the curve of the skull, flowing just under the top, then to the back and down into the neck. It continues straight down the left, red channel to the three-channel junction, about four finger widths below the navel.

Pause there for few seconds and, still holding the breath, move the right ring finger over to close the left nostril. Imagine the air now entering the right, white channel at the junction.

Now exhale using the nine-breath release, pushing the air up through the channel and clearing it by releasing any static, blockages, or obscurations.

Imagine the air leaving the right nostril as black smoke representing the stale, polluted inner energy of air related to aversion. This poison includes all forms of resistance or pushing away. It ranges from anger, resentment, and hurt feelings to avoidance and denial behaviors and the extreme forms of hatred and violence.

Pause for a few seconds to sense some clearing and refreshing. Now repeat this process for a total of three full breaths.

THE SECOND SET OF THREE BREATHS

Raise your left hand with the thumb pressing against the middle of the ring finger. Now close your left nostril with the tip of that ring finger. Inhale slowly and deeply through your right nostril. Imagine you are breathing in pure green light.

As before, imagine the air rising up the nostril, passing just behind the right eye, then following the curve of the skull, flowing just under the top, then to the back and down into the neck. It continues straight down the right, white channel to the three-channel junction, about four finger widths below the navel.

Pause there for a few seconds and move the left ring finger over to close the right nostril. The air now enters the left, red channel at the junction and will clear that channel as it is expelled.

Using the nine-breath release, push the air up through the red channel, releasing any static, blockages, or obscurations. Imagine the air leaving the left nostril as black smoke representing the stale, polluted inner energy of air related to attachment or greed. This poison includes all forms of grasping, holding, and being mentally stuck. It ranges from egocentric and controlling behaviors to extreme forms of desire and addiction.

Pause for a few seconds to sense some clearing and refreshing. Now repeat this process for a total of three full breaths.

THE THIRD SET OF THREE BREATHS

Clearing the gross afflictions associated with the side channels makes way for the ultimate purpose of the nine-breath purification—clearing the central channel.

Of all the energetic pathways in the body, our central channel is the most important because it is the seat of our rigpa; our buddha nature.

The heart chakra resides at the center of the central channel. It hosts the palace of primordial pure awareness.

It is ignorance, the root of all affliction, that is cleared from the central channel. This is the ignorance of not knowing the true nature of reality and holding an incorrect view of self and other.

Ignorance manifests in all forms of disconnection from one's essence, ranging from a lack of self-awareness, self-confidence, and self-understanding to extreme forms of indifference, indecision, and confusion.

To begin this set of breaths, rest your hands on your knees or fold them together just under the navel in the classic equipoise position. Now breathe in fully and deeply through both nostrils. Imagine you are breathing in glistening, white, healing light. Pull it down both side channels to the three-channel junction and hold it there as long as you can.

Take this holding time to send the healing energy of breath throughout your body, especially into areas that are weak, damaged, diseased, or in pain. When holding becomes a bit uncomfortable, use the nine-breath release directed up through the central blue channel and out the crown. Imagine the air leaving as pink light[13] representing the stale, polluted inner energy of air related to ignorance.

Pause for a moment and rest in the feeling of clarity and renewal. Now repeat this process for a total of three breaths.

NINE-BREATH DAILY PRACTICE

Even if you have little time for a spiritual practice at the start of your day, try to take a few minutes to do the nine-breath meditation. You're already breathing, so just do it more mindfully, as directed in this exercise, and see what a difference those few minutes will make in your day.

It is also advisable to do this practice whenever situations occur or emotions arise that throw you off balance. Learn to acknowledge those times and, instead of reacting or losing control emotionally, take just five minutes and perform the nine-breath meditation.

If you are truly pressed for time, shorten the practice to one breath per channel. In a split-second emergency, take one deep central channel breath and let it go with the nine-breath release exhalation.

As you gain familiarity with this practice, you will see that it makes a positive difference in how your day unfolds. It could actually save your life, your relationship, your mind, your health. In light of that, is there any good reason not to practice?

Ignore the surface mind that says, "Later, I'm in a hurry," or "I have more important things to do." Listen to your inner awareness that knows the long-term benefits of this simple, short exercise. It will definitely be a benefit for yourself and others, even if the benefit is not obvious at first. Never think that you are wasting time in meditation practice.

PART V

Breath and Movement

15. The Body–Mind Connection

With the breath, body and mind connect
immediately.
With the breath, compassion and wisdom unite
naturally.
With the breath, relative and ultimate truth combine
"as it is."
With the breath, mindfulness and awareness join
as a team.
With the breath, self and other merge
into one.

YOU'VE PROBABLY NOTICED that your state of mind affects your body and the way you breathe. For example, when you're agitated, your blood pressure, heart rate, and muscle tension increase, and your breathing becomes fast and shallow. When you're feeling happy and peaceful, your body relaxes, and your breathing becomes slower and deeper.

Just as your state of mind affects your body and the way you breathe, your physical condition and the way you breathe affects your mind. Because body and mind mirror each other in this way, you can create an intentional feedback loop where one guides the other back into balance.

Breath is a bridge that makes this possible. Even during times of acute emotion, such as weeping, fear, or anger, taking a few deep breaths will immediately calm things down physically, which calms the mind and opens it to a wider perspective.

PARTNERS

Body and mind are bound in this life as partners. Just like humans, they can live within the same space and yet appear to be almost unconscious of each other, or they can be attentive, appreciative, and respectful of each other.

In a good body–mind relationship, the partners are responsive, engaged, and connected. They know each other fully and understand each other's feelings, needs, and expressions. The strength of their partnership lies in the way they support and serve each other.

The biggest problem that creeps into partnerships is the erosion of good communication, and the biggest problem that creeps into effective communication is an inability or unwillingness to listen.

Over time, partners may slip into patterns of disconnection: making assumptions, creating expectations, taking things for granted, avoiding problems, or pushing their own agendas. As the distance between them grows, it's more difficult to see and act on signs of trouble. When communication becomes blocked, the relationship becomes marked by "dis-ease" and suffering.

Our well-being depends on how our body and mind relate. We are free to neglect this partnership, inviting all kinds of physical pain and illness and all kinds of mental stress and neurosis. We are also free to choose a vibrant, healthy life by taking the time to nurture the body–mind relationship through awareness.

It is easy to see the incredible power and potential of the mind, but it is also important to recognize the complexity and intelligence of the body. Thoughts, memories, and emotions are not just held in the head, they are carried in the body as well.

For example, resentment may be manufactured in the mind, but it will run through the body like a toxic chemical, stressing the heart, tensing muscles, and even changing the facial expression.

Yoga, tai chi, and qigong are a few examples of the many mind-training methods used around the world that include breath and body movement to restore and maintain the balance and flow of energy in the body and mind.

The following are two exercises that strengthen the body–mind connection. The first one is done in stillness, with the mind's full attention trained on the body. The second one is done by synchronizing the breath with body movements to release physical and mental tension, inviting the mind to "come home," clear, alert, and refreshed.

BODY SCAN

This exercise is done while sitting still. It is a method for coming into the present moment by being fully aware of and present with your body, as it is.

Take a moment to enter a rhythm of deep, calm, relaxing breaths. When you feel settled, mentally scan your body, moving inch by inch from the top of your head to the bottom of your feet. Learn to sense exactly where you are in the body. Release any tension as you go, moving slowly down the skull, face, neck, shoulders, arms, and hands; then down the torso, hips, legs, and feet.

Notice any sensations that come up as you travel past all the landmarks (muscles, joints, spine, organs, etc.). Without any mental comment, judgment, or resistance, check to see whether feelings in each area are pleasant, painful, or neutral.

Usually, we react to even the smallest amount of pain with impatience and rejection. We just want to get rid of it. When something feels pleasant, we try to hang onto it and make it last or we try to re-live it.

The problem is that the more we try to push pain away, the more it settles in; and the harder we try to keep our pleasant sensations, the faster they disappear.

In this exercise, we simply notice and let things be. Amazingly, in that environment of acceptance and awareness, what was viewed as pain or pleasure transforms into what is neutral. In this space, the body naturally balances and heals itself and the bliss of equanimity arises.

BRINGING THE MIND HOME; LETTING GO

The purpose of this exercise is to relax and refresh body and mind. It is done while standing. The in-breath is taken while physically standing up tall and mentally bringing the mind and awareness home.

The out-breath is released in two bursts while physically bending over, doing two "bouncing" knee bends, and mentally letting go of all problems, worries, and attachments.

Here is the sequence in more detail:

To Start

As you take a long, deep breath, open your chest, and bending the elbows, lift your hands (turned down) up to shoulder height.

Exhale

Bounce 1: As you release the first breath, lean forward and bend the knees slightly as you drop down into the first down-and-up bounce. As you "hit the bottom" of the down part of the bounce, air is naturally forced out of the lungs. Feel the release and mentally say, "Letting go."

At the same time as you are dropping down, let your arms also drop down and swing to the back. You then naturally bounce up slightly, completing the first bounce. At this point you are still leaning over and the arms are extended behind you.

Bounce 2: Let the arms naturally swing forward just in front of you while your knees drop down into another bend and up again—blowing out more air at the bottom of that bend.

INHALE AND STRETCH

Inhale deeply as you stand up straight and continue to swing the extended arms up, over, and slightly behind your head. Mentally say, "Bringing the mind home."

If you can't stretch your arms up fully, just bring them back to the starting position, just in front of the shoulders.

REPEAT

Now repeat the sequence, exhaling again while dropping the arms down and swinging them to the back while bouncing down and up on knees, as before, and returning to the full upright position.

Do this twenty-one times for one set. Between sets make sure you take a break, breathing in and out at least five times before the next set.

This exercise (and its variation, described below) is typically done before sitting in a formal meditation session. It is a great way to clear the mind, strengthen the body, release tension, and generate positive energy. It is especially helpful to do when you are stressed out or feeling dull from being inside or sitting too long.

VARIATION: OFFERING, BLESSING, RELEASING

Once you are familiar with the exercise above, it can be adapted to serve as a classic prostration:

- As you inhale and stretch, lift your arms with your palms up and imagine offering the best of your life and the world.
- With your arms fully extended overhead, bring your palms together.
- As the hands separate and start to drop down, imagine receiving the blessing of exactly what you need right now.
- As you exhale with the knee-bends, swinging the arms back and forth, imagine completely relaxing and releasing everything that is holding you back or is no longer needed in your life.

16. The Five Magic Movements

Butter is always within the milk.
Without churning, it won't appear.
Wisdom and healing can happen
when awareness and vital energy are generated.

TSA LUNG TRUL KHOR is the Tibetan name for special exercises that promote health and healing by purifying and balancing the five root *lungs*, or wind energies. As described in chapter 3, these are known as the upward moving, life-force, fire-like, pervasive, and downward clearing winds. Each exercise is a blend of breathing and body movements that are performed while visualizing the movement of energy.

Tsa refers to energy channels within the body, *lung* refers to energy and breath, *trul* means magic, and *khor* refers to a moving wheel (chakra). These simple, unified movements of body, breath, and energy are so powerful that they are referred to as magic. The health benefits of *tsa lung trul khor* have been demonstrated scientifically and the exercises are now being used as a healing modality in several hospitals and universities. They are truly wonderful tools for relieving physical and emotional struggles and pain.

There is one basic *tsa lung trul khor* exercise for each root *lung*. Each exercise is carried out in five steps:

1. *Sit* comfortably in the five-point posture.
2. *Inhale and hold* the breath in a specific chakra within the body.
3. *Exercise* using physical movement.

4. *Inhale a little more* and continue to hold.

5. *Exhale* using the nine-breath release.

During the third step, each movement is typically repeated five times to the right and five times to the left (constituting one set) during one breath-hold. However, to avoid running out of breath, beginners should start with only three movements to the right and three to the left. For the same reason, they should focus on the main movement described until it can be done with ease. Then the additional movement mentioned can be included.

Adding more breath in the fourth step is like sealing or putting a lid on the breath. You then rest in equipoise, completely relaxed, while focusing on the energy and chakra related to the exercise. Remain in this meditation as long as you can until you feel the need to breathe again. Do not force the breath-hold.

In between each set of movements, the practitioner should take a break for least forty-five seconds. Take this time to completely let go of struggles and attachments and rest with body and mind in their natural state.[14]

UPWARD MOVING WIND EXERCISE

Although this energy is flowing and functioning everywhere in the body, its main activity is in the throat and up through the face, head, and crown. This is why it is called upward moving, or *gyen gyu* in Tibetan. Speaking and breathing in and out are activities of *gyen gyu lung* energy but its primary function is to open the five senses and the throat and crown chakras, which refreshes the brain and increases intellectual capacity. This exercise helps carry away the physical discomfort of headaches or heaviness in the head. It also helps release judgmental and negative thoughts.

1. Sit comfortably in the five-point posture.

2. Inhale slowly, gently, and fully through both nostrils, directing

the breath down the side channels to their junction, just below the navel. Now, imagine the breath rising up through the central energy channel to the throat chakra. Hold your breath and attention there.

3. *Main Movement:* Relax your neck, drop your head forward and down, and gently roll it to the right (clockwise) in a full circle. Do five rotations. As you do them, imagine the upward moving flow of energy through your head as you are rotating it. Then reverse the motion and do five rotations to the left (anti-clockwise).

Additional Movement: If you can still hold your breath, proceed to drop the head forward and then tip it back, five times. Beginners may need to skip this part.

4. Breathe in a little more and continue to hold.

5. Exhale using the nine-breath release. Imagine that all blockages and *lung* imbalances in the throat, head, and crown chakras are

carried on the breath and expelled out of the body through the crown chakra. This completes one set.

Take a break for at least forty-five seconds and then repeat the entire exercise two more times for a total of three sets.

Note: When you are learning this exercise, and at the beginning of the practice, start with a small, careful, circular motion, and if possible, work up to a full, relaxed, rolling motion. The movement should always be very gentle and soft. The exercise itself will help increase your range of motion and keep the neck limber. Keep the circular neck motion as small as necessary to avoid any pain or discomfort.

LIFE-FORCE WIND EXERCISE

Although it can be everywhere in the body, the main seat of life-force energy is in the heart. This energy brings confidence, strength, success, fulfilment, joy, vitality, and compassion.

1. Sit comfortably in the five-point posture with your hands on your hips.
2. Breathe in slowly, gently, and fully through both nostrils, directing the breath down the side channels to their junction, just below the navel. Now, imagine the breath rising up through the central channel to the heart chakra. Hold your breath and attention there.
3. *Main Movement:* Start with your hands on your hips.

Now, as though throwing a lasso, lift your right arm up, stretching it out in front of you and pass your open hand over the left side of your head, around behind the head, and around to the right.

As you complete this circular motion, close your hand into a fist. At this point, it is beside your right ear.

Now throw your hand out, either to your right side or in front of you. As you throw, open your fingers wide.

Repeat the lasso movement three or five times. Then do the same movement three or five times on the left side using the left arm.

Additional Movement: If you can still hold your breath, proceed to rotate the right shoulder (forward, up, back, and down) three or five times. As the shoulder moves forward, move it as far as possible in front of you, rotating the rib cage and heart chakra to the left. Now repeat the rotations using the left shoulder.

4. Breathe in a little more and continue to hold.
5. Exhale through the nostrils using the nine-breath release. Imagine that all the blockages and *lung* imbalances in the heart, lungs,

chest, and upper body are carried on the breath and expelled. This exercise helps clear emotional troubles, especially feelings of hurt and resentment.

Take a break for at least forty-five seconds, then repeat the entire exercise for a total of three sets.

FIRE-LIKE WIND EXERCISE

Although fire-like *lung* energy moves and acts throughout the body, its main location is the navel chakra or stomach area. It supports digestion, purifies toxic food, and distributes nutrition. It also supports inner peace and comfort.

1. Sit comfortably in the five-point posture with your right hand on your right knee and your left hand on your left knee.
2. Breath in slowly, gently, and fully through both nostrils, directing the breath down the side channels to their junction, just below the navel. Now imagine the breath rising up through the central channel to the navel area itself. Focus on this center of glowing energy and wisdom or awareness.

   Lock that energy in place by tightening muscles from above and below. This is done by pulling the muscles of the perineum and anus up toward the navel while, at the same time, pressing down toward the navel with muscles of the stomach and diaphragm. Hold your breath and attention here.
3. *Main Movement:* Still squeezing the muscles all around the glowing center, slowly and gently rotate it as around a vertical axis, five times to the right (clockwise). Stop and then repeat by rotating it five times to the left (counter-clockwise).
4. Breathe in a little more and continue to hold.
5. Exhale through the nostrils using the nine-breath release. Imagine that all the blockages and *lung* imbalances of the navel chakra and the internal organs, especially the liver and kidneys, are expelled

and carried away on the breath. Also imagine that the wisdom fire has burned away ignorance and confusion.

Additional Movement: If you can still hold your breath, proceed to pump the stomach in and out five times. Push it out in front of you, then squeeze it back in toward the spine. Beginners may need to skip this part.

Take a break for at least forty-five seconds, then repeat the entire exercise for a total of three sets.

PERVASIVE WIND EXERCISE

Pervasive *lung* energy can be anywhere and everywhere in the body, but it is mainly located within the arms, legs, and head, which are referred to as the five limbs. It flows with a vital, energizing power that increases the ability to take on multiple roles and accomplish many things. This energy supports flexibility and lightness of body while bringing strength and healing to muscles, joints, and the brain.

1. Sit comfortably in the five-point posture.
2. Breathe in slowly, gently, and fully through both nostrils, directing the breath down the side channels to their junction, just below the navel. Now, send that energy all over your body, especially through all five limbs. Hold your breath and attention on this energy that is in and around you, everywhere.
3. *Main Movement:* Clap your hands loudly in front of you and then

rub them together vigorously, about five to seven times, until you feel heat.

Imagine that this rubbing is generating the wisdom energy you need to wash away negative karmic traces and emotions. The washing is done throughout the rest of the movement, which is like rubbing or massaging your body from top to bottom, as described below.

After generating wisdom heat in your hands, extend your right arm in front of you and put your left hand on the top back of your right hand. Rub up the top side of your arm to the shoulder and back down again.

Now rub up the underside of your arm to the armpit and back down again. Switch arms and repeat these movements on the other side.

Still holding your breath, complete one long, flowing, massaging movement from the top of your head to the tip of your feet. Start by placing both hands on the back of your head. Now wipe or pull your open, flat palms over the top of your head, then down over your forehead, eyes, and face.

Continue down over the front of your torso, then up and down over the back and sides, and down over your hips.

Now stretch out your right leg while bringing both hands over to the top of that thigh, wrapping them around it as much as possible.

The movement continues by sweeping or pushing your hands down the thigh, over the knee, shin, and on to the tip of your foot, then all the way back up to the top of your thigh. Repeat on the left leg.

Additional Movement: This is an action like shooting with a bow and arrow. The arrow represents your negative emotions, blockages, and karmic traces. Start with your fists almost touching just in front of your chest. Turn your eyes and head toward the right. Imagine you are holding the bow with your right hand and pulling the arrow back with your left.

Now pull your hands wide apart to either side of you. As you do this, toss your right hand out, wide open, signifying the release of the arrow and all of your negativities. Imagine that the arrow carries those negativities thousands of miles away from you. Do this bow and arrow move three or five times on each side.

4. Breathe in a little more and continue to hold.
5. Exhale through the nostrils using the nine-breath release. Imagine that all the emotional blockages and *lung* imbalances of the head and the entire body are carried away on the breath and expelled.

Take a break for at least forty-five seconds, then repeat the entire exercise for a total of three sets.

DOWNWARD CLEARING WIND EXERCISE

Downward clearing energy can be everywhere within the body, but it is mainly located in the abdominal area that houses the bladder, colon, and sexual organs. This *lung* energy can bring pleasure and healing in the lower body. Its activity results in cleansing through the processes of elimination. Downward clearing wind energy also supports inner calmness and stability.

1. Sit comfortably in the five-point posture.
2. Breathe in slowly, gently, and fully through both nostrils, directing the breath down the side channels to their junction, just below the navel. Now hold your breath and attention at the bottom or secret place chakra. Pull up the perineum and pelvic floor, gently holding these muscles up throughout the exercise.
3. *Main Movement* Begin by grasping your right knee with both hands. Drop your torso and head down over that knee and make a low, wide circle to the left, over the left knee, then around toward the back and into an upright position again.

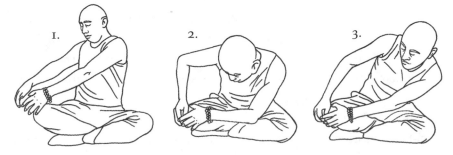

Use the knee as a brace, pushing it down as you lean over it, then pulling it up slightly as you rise into the sitting position.

Complete three or five rotations and change sides. Grab the left knee with both hands, leaning your torso and head over the left knee, and make a low, wide circle to the right. Complete three or five rotations.

Additional Movement: If you can still hold your breath, this last set of rotations will be done with both knees pulled up about halfway off the floor, ankles crossed. Begin by holding the top of your right knee with your right hand and the top of your left knee with your left hand.

Now let your right knee lift up as you push down on the left knee (which shifts the weight of your left hip bone onto the floor) while twisting and rotating your pelvis to the right.

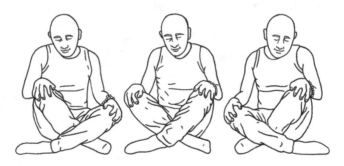

Now switch, lifting your left knee and pushing down on the right (shifting the weight of your right bottom bone onto the floor) while twisting and rotating your pelvis to the left.

Although you remain in one spot, the shifting weight is like walking on the floor with your hip bones.

The center or hub of this circular, rocking movement is the secret chakra located at the very bottom of your torso. It ends up moving in a small, circular path.

4. Breathe in a little more and continue to hold.

5. Exhale through the nostrils using the nine-breath release. Imagine

that all the blockages and *lung* imbalances of the secret place chakra and lower body, organs, and doors are carried on the breath and expelled. Also imagine that any negative emotions related to attachment, greed, and depression are released.

Take a break for at least forty-five seconds, then repeat the entire exercise for a total of three sets.

Note: If you are sitting on a cushion, it is best to remove it and sit flat on the floor for these exercises.

If you have bad knees or are a beginner, be very careful not to strain your knees. For the main movement, you may need to adjust the knee position by lifting them up high, but try to keep your ankles crossed with the sides of your feet on the floor.

PART VI

Breath and Sound

17. Mantra: The Voice of Meditation

Mantra is the language of god and spirit.
Mantra is the voice of your own energy.
Mantra is the inspiration of spiritual journey.
Mantra is the power of healing and protection.
Mantra is the essence of breath and intention.

AT THE MOST FUNDAMENTAL LEVEL, everything in and around us is vibrational energy. In its original form, this energy arises out of empty space as primordial sound (*da*), light (*öd*), and rays (*ser*). These three are described by qualities related to their "self" nature.

The Tibetan word for self is *rang*. The three primordial energies are called *rang shar* or "self-arising." They emerge spontaneously and completely on their own from the great mother—the vast, clear space from which all phenomena are born.

They are also called *rang trol* or self-liberating because they spontaneously liberate themselves, dissolving back into the empty space from which they came.

Sound, light, and rays are called *rang da*, *rang öd*, and *rang ser*; self-sound, self-light, and self-rays. They are described as "self" not only because they are self-arising and self-liberating but also because they are none other than our true self. They are the source of our physical voice, mind, and body. In the Dzogchen view, they are naturally pure and perfect. Discovering them through spiritual practice is discovering who we really are.

It is important to understand that the sounds, lights, and forms we experience are not coming from somewhere else; they are our essential nature. Recognizing this after death is particularly crucial for the ultimate liberation of our consciousness during the transitional period known as the *bardo*.[15]

In this intermediate state, if we are familiar with our energetic nature, we are less likely to be disturbed or thrown off track by the sounds, lights, and forms that can manifest in intensely beautiful and horrifying ways. Instead of being blocked and swept away by them in fear, desire, and confusion, we can recognize that they are arising from our own innate awareness and open the door to enlightenment.

RANG DA

There are trillions of sounds inside of us but we don't hear them because our mind is too distracted and overwhelmed by all of the sounds around us. This is like not being able to see the stars during the day—they're still there but the sun outshines them.

In our normal dualistic ego state of mind we don't hear the self-sound that is the nature of all the sounds. As with our other senses, perceiving (in this case hearing) is immediately followed by creating associations, interpretations, and fabrications.

There is a Bön practice called *mun tsam* that helps practitioners realize their innate, self-arising, and self-liberating nature—including that inner, self-manifesting sound that is inseparable from the inherent self-sound of the universe. This is the traditional dark retreat practice where all the external sense doors are effectively closed by remaining in complete darkness, stillness, and silence for up to forty-nine days. The retreat is done under the guidance of a master and with organized support for the delivery of food and water through special light-proof slots.

MANTRA

According to Bön teachings, we can use our breath and the sound of our own voice to deeply connect to ourselves, to others, and to primordial awareness itself. This is done by sounding the sacred syllables or mantras created and given to us by enlightened beings for our benefit. The full meaning and power of a mantra comes through reciting or chanting it.

The vibrational energy of our cells, nerves, tissues, muscles, and organs can become diminished, disturbed, or distorted. If the damage is persistent and widespread, our entire life force can be affected.

Because mantras carry the same energy that is the foundation of our body and mind, they can help restore our vibrational frequencies by bringing them into line with their own.

Different mantras have different energetic frequencies and are used for different purposes. Some are used for healing specific diseases or parts of the body. Some connect us to specific enlightened qualities. Some unblock and open specific energy channels or chakras.

Once sounded, it is believed that the vibrations of the mantra continue to flow out indefinitely. This reminds me of the songs of whales that travel through the ocean for hundreds and even thousands of miles.

Some mantras are recited in one tone, and some are chanted or sung with specific melodies. With all of them, the movement of breath and the mouth is considered to be very important. That is why, if chanting must be done quietly, it is better to whisper it through moving lips than to just repeat it mentally.

We can see how everyday music can change our feelings, emotions, and energy level. Music can be exciting and uplifting, liberating the vital energy of our body and mind. It can make us smile, laugh, jump, and dance; it can also bring us to tears and sadness.

Like good music, reciting mantras generates positive energy and well-being. There is no limit to the power of mantric sound when we direct it from our heart using our breath and voice.

CHANTING EXPERIENCES

It was my grandmother who first taught me to recite mantras. I remember saying healing mantras when I was sick. It always worked. Even if I couldn't eat or swallow from a sore throat, when I recited the mantra, the illness dissolved.

Since then, I have experienced many memorable moments while chanting mantras that have reinforced my trust in their power to influence body, mind, and spirit.

For example, I was asked to chant a number of times during different parts of a large funeral service. When the service was over, a young pregnant lady came running up to me to exclaim that every time I chanted, her baby started "dancing" and kicking inside. When I stopped chanting, the baby stopped moving. The mother felt sure her baby was responding to the energy and vibration of the mantra.

Another time, a young couple asked me to bless their newborn baby. The precious little one was sleeping in a basket with her head tipped over to the side. I stood quite a few feet away and was very careful not to wake her. It is common, at the end of the chanting, to send the full power and blessing of the mantra to the recipient by gently blowing a breath through the lips toward him or her. As I did this from a distance, the baby turned her head up and shuddered all over, then drifted back into a deep sleep. Her parents were amazed at the response.

Once I was traveling by taxi with a friend who had recently been stung on the arm by a jellyfish. His arm was blistered and he was in a lot of pain. I chanted a healing mantra and, as with the newborn baby, blew a blessing at the end, but this time directly on his arm. My friend looked down and then yelled to the driver to check his arm out now. The area was covered in goose bumps, the wound looked completely different, and he felt better, immediately.

Repeating sacred mantras is something you can always do for yourself and others, no matter what situation you might find yourself in.

It supports, soothes, and stabilizes even in the toughest moments of suffering, tragedy, death, and grief.

MANTRA OF THE LOVING MOTHER

A heart mantra captures and connects us to the essence, depth, and power of specific enlightened qualities. One of the most cherished mantras in my tradition is that of the wisdom-loving mother, the Sherab Chamma Heart Mantra. She is is the female archetype of wisdom and compassion, very similar to Tara, Quan Yin, or the Virgin Mary. Her heart mantra is a string of twenty-one syllables, each one symbolizing the different qualities of one of her twenty-one manifestations:

> OM MA WA MA DE MA HI MO HA
> E MA HO MA YE RU PA YE TA DU-DU SO HA

A number of years ago, I sent a recording of me chanting the Sherab Chamma Heart Mantra to a friend. My friend started crying as soon as he heard it and wept for four days. As he listened, again and again, many old wounds were surfacing and clearing. At first, he didn't know what the mantra was. When I explained, he was able to make connections to his own mother and other female buddhas that were prominent in his life. For him, the mantra was a powerful source of healing.

He ended up creating a video from my recording and posted it online. Another man in Switzerland saw the video from his deathbed in a hospital. As he listened to it again and again, he got better and better until he was able to return home. Eventually, he tracked me down and described how the mantra had saved his life.

The Sherab Chamma Heart Mantra has a particularly beautiful melody. As we sing it again and again, the wisdom, compassion, and fearlessness of the loving mother can manifest in us and around us through the people and circumstances of our lives.[16]

MANTRAS AND PRAYER FLAGS

Whenever I find myself on a mountain or beside the ocean, I recite mantras and then softly blow out the energy of the mantras from my mouth into the space around me.

Just as mantras can be carried on our breath, we can imagine them being carried on the breath of wind. *Lung ta*, as I mentioned in chapter 6, is the mythical wind horse that rises on the wind to carry the energy of the mantra and deliver it wherever it is needed in the world.

Both mantras and the *lung ta* image are printed on Tibetan prayer flags that are hung in long strings on mountain tops, high hills, house fronts, trees, or any other place where they will be moved by the energy of wind. Higher elevations are prized for prayer flags, as the energy associated with the flags is considered to be more powerful there.

The practice of hanging Tibetan prayer flags was started by Bönpos (Bön practitioners) more than two thousand years ago. At that time, the country was ruled by warlords who carried their banners into battles. The indigenous Bönpos, however, made their own flags to honor the spirits of the natural world. They hung them over mountain passes and rivers to benefit all who would pass underneath.

The colors of the flags and the symbolic animals printed on them represent the five elements: white/snow lion for space, green/horse for air, red/garuda for fire, blue/dragon for water, and yellow/tiger for earth.

The wind horse at the center of each flag carries the blessings of love and compassion to all sentient beings throughout the universe. The blessings are represented by the *norbu*, or precious wish-fulfilling treasure, on its back.

As wind passes over the surface of the flags, the air is purified and energized by the sacred mantras that are printed on them. This is a powerful method for cultivating compassion that is used whenever possible in the Tibetan culture.

This Bön prayer flag, from Samling Monastery in the remote Himalayan region of Dolpo, is housed at the Rubin Museum of Art in New York City. There are four prayers or mantras written across the flag: the five warrior seed syllables; the 'sale öd' wisdom mantra; the five elements mantra; and an aspirational prayer for increasing the five basic energies (life force, health, prosperity, reputation, and soul or mental confidence).

18. Seed Syllables

As we chant,
the breath becomes the voice,
the singer becomes the listener,
the sound becomes the appearance
of enlightened qualities, and
we become one with our true nature.

A SEED SYLLABLE is a sacred sound, full of meaning and energy, that serves as a direct connection to the source of all. In Tibetan, as with all seeds, it is called *sabon*, or seed of the ground.

SOUND AS SEED

Like the seed of a plant, a seed syllable is the source or foundation of life. It is a coded, concentrated form of energy that holds the potential for the manifestation of unique forms and appearances. It is a seed of becoming.

Under the right conditions, a tiny plant seed will completely transform into all of the complexities unique to an individual plant. The plant will then generate hundreds of seeds that will go on to generate thousands more, until countless manifestations have emerged from the one source. This is a good analogy for the limitless potential of expression held within a seed syllable.

Each seed syllable is depicted by a sacred letter that symbolizes the specific enlightened qualities related to that sound. Some syllables and related mantras can be translated into meaningful language and some cannot. Ultimately, their essence is beyond thinking and common words, carried within pure, original sound itself.

In Tibetan Bönpo understanding, just as there are countless living beings around us, there are also countless deities or buddhas. The essence of each one is represented by his or her own seed syllable. The process of visualizing enlightened ones and connecting to their qualities starts with visualizing and chanting their seed syllable.

For example, a formal Sherab Chamma practice includes reciting the *choka*,[17] or pages of prayers from a ritual text. Before that begins, her form and qualities are invoked by repeating her seed syllable.[18] That sound is the foundation of her enlightened manifestation. Her appearance arises from and goes back into the ground that holds the seed.

A mantra may be made of one or many seed syllables. *Sung ngak*, the Tibetan phrase for "mantra," means we say it or sing it. In doing so, we activate the energy concentrated within it and the conditions necessary for the seed to germinate and grow.

Sounding seed syllables with an open heart and a focused mind connects us back to our source. As we chant, the breath becomes the voice, the singer becomes the listener, the sound becomes the appearance of enlightened qualities, and we become one with our true nature.

THE FIVE WARRIOR SEED SYLLABLES

AH   OM   HUNG   RAM   DZA

There are five primordial sounds that are considered the source of all other sounds, mantras, and miraculous letters of the alphabet.[19] They are called *pawo dru nga*, or the five warrior seed syllables; *pawo* means "warrior," *dru* means "seed," and *nga* means "five."

According to the Bön tradition, these sounds were discovered and given to us by the founder of Bön, Tönpa Shenrab, a buddha who walked the earth many thousands of years before Buddha Shakyamuni. There is a great mythological story of how this came about:

One year, while Tönpa Shenrab was teaching far from home, a famous trickster, the demon Khyabpa, convinced Tönpa Shenrab's daughter, Shensa Neuchung, that they should burn his most sacred text to get his attention and make him come home. The knowledge in this text was hidden in precious sacred symbols.

Like all buddhas, Tönpa Shenrab had the clairvoyance of wisdom and knew what was happening, but he didn't return home until the deed was done.

He then went to the place where the precious text had been burned and bent down, putting his hands in the ashes. Everything was completely burned up save for five indestructible syllables he lifted from the soot.

Then, an amazing thing happened. A ball of rainbow light came down upon him, and out of the light, writing paper materialized that was as white as a bleached conch shell.

Again, the rainbow light descended, and out of it came a beautiful golden pen. Finally, the light delivered a flask of the most amazing turquoise ink.

It was clear what he was to do. Using the five indestructible syllables as a foundation, he created and recorded forty letters that humanity could use for learning, writing, and reading. The letters are known as *trul yig zhichu*, where *trul* means "magic," *yig* means "letters," and *zhichu* means "forty"—the forty magic letters. They include all the marks and symbols of the Tibetan alphabet that are still in use today.

The original five syllables are seen as the source of all knowledge and wisdom. They are described as warriors for the way they defend, protect, and overcome all "demons," or negative forces. They symbolize protection from outer destructive forces such as fire and water, inner threats to physical health, and secret mental and emotional turmoil.

In the Tibetan culture, the creative power of the five original syllables is acknowledged every time a sacred image, *thangka*, or statue is blessed. This is done by writing or inserting the syllables at their respective chakra sites along an imagined central energy channel. It is believed that this process breathes consciousness and life into otherwise inanimate, empty objects.

FROM AH TO DZA

From AH to DZA, the five warrior qualities are interdependent and arise in a foundational order, starting with space. Space, as the ground of all being, is empty of anything in particular and full of all potential. It is inherently clear, open, and luminous.

Space is like a clear blue sky with the nurturing warmth of the sun beating down. If the sky is obscured by clouds, there is little chance to see the sun or feel its warmth.

In the same way, the space within us (AH) can be obscured by thoughts and emotions. As it clouds over, the clear light (OM) of our wisdom and awareness fades and we lose our capacity to be loving, compassionate, joyful, and at peace (HUNG). This situation drains us of energy and vitality (RAM). Then, beneficial activity (DZA) that used to flow effortlessly and spontaneously becomes a struggle marked by frustration and disappointment. The more effort we exert trying to make things better, the more drained we become.

This order of causality works in reverse as well. When our behavior and actions (DZA) are not in accord with our essence, our vitality (RAM) becomes depleted. As our energy drains, we're more likely to become preoccupied with our own problems and less able to see the suffering of others or be moved by compassion and loving kindness (HUNG). This causes the clear light of our awareness (OM) to diminish, making it more difficult to see and experience the open space (AH) of our true nature that is now hidden from view by the clouds of negative thoughts, emotions, and consequences of our actions.

Syllable	Sound	Light/Color	Quality	Chakra
ཨ	AH	white	infinite space, emptiness	crown: great bliss
ཨོཾ	OM	red	clear light, wisdom	throat: enjoyment
ཧཱུྃ	HUNG	blue	love/compassion, joy/equanimity	heart: emptiness
རཾ	RAM	red	energy/strength, vitality	navel: manifestation
ཛཿ	DZA	green	effortless beneficial activity	bottom or secret: generating bliss

SACRED ART

One way to become familiar with the five warrior seed syllables is to practice writing them in calligraphy. I first learned to trace them out in ashes at the bottom of a box, as writing supplies were extremely limited in the monastery.

Calligraphy practice is meditation. It is a way to focus the mind while opening up creativity and consciousness itself. It can also be a way to connect and make offerings to the five elements from which everything arises.

For example, drawing seed syllables in the space in front of you is a way of making an offering to the spirit of the space element. In one gesture, you, the syllable, its qualities, and the element are unified.

Drawing sacred seed syllables on prayer flags to be carried on *lung ta* is making an offering to the wind element. Sketching them on paper and burning the paper in a fire is making an offering to the spirit of the fire element. Tracing them in the sand at the beach is a way of making an offering to both the earth and the water elements, as the waves will eventually take them away. Carving them in stone or simply tracing them on the ground is a way of paying homage to the earth element.

Bönpos believe that acknowledging the elements in this way generates peace, harmony, and healing. It also serves to protect, free, and open the heart and mind.

The following chapter includes a breakdown of separate strokes used to draw each seed syllable. The stroke sequence follows the basic order of Tibetan calligraphy: top to bottom and left to right.

Once you know how to make the basic shapes with a pencil or pen, you can try a more artful form using a beveled felt-tip marker or the traditional paint and flat brush. And don't forget the freedom and fun of drawing them into the elements with the invisible ink of your imagination.

19. Connecting to Five Warrior Qualities

Tönpa Shenrab
placed a message upon the breath,
our messenger,
whispering of the five warrior qualities
carried within everyone, equally,
delivering a choice:
Will you connect to them or not?

THERE IS A FATHOMLESS DEPTH of meaning in each of the five warrior seed syllables. Following are a few of the most basic aspects of each syllable:

AH IS INFINITE SPACE

ཨཿ

AH is the seed syllable for the space element. Its vibrational energy is associated with white light and the chakra at the crown of our head.

When we sound AH, we connect to the vast, pure, open, changeless qualities of infinite space:

> AH is Vast,
> Beyond all boundaries and limitations.
>
> AH is Pure,
> Beginningless and perfect,
> beyond disturbance or notions of good and bad.
>
> AH is Open,
> Completely free and spacious with room for
> all possibility and potential.
>
> AH is Changeless.
> It is as it is; the stable seat of the universe.
>
> When you are space, nothing can harm you.

Stroke sequence for drawing AH:

OM IS CLEAR LIGHT

OM is the seed syllable for the light of awareness that dwells in space. Its vibrational energy is related to red light and to the throat chakra.

When we sound OM, we empower speech and connect to the clear light of our wisdom-awareness:

OM is Pure,
Beyond all obstruction, fabrication, and confusion.

OM is Luminous,
Vivid and vibrant,
illuminating direct perception.

OM is Awareness,
Knowing, seeing, hearing, realizing, accepting all.

OM is Empowered Speech,
Fluent, direct, clear, and effective,
dynamic, unceasing expression.

Stroke sequence for drawing OM:

ཨ ཨྲ ཨྲ ཨྲུ ཨྲུ ཨོྲུ ཨཱོྲུ ཨཱོྃྲུ

HUNG IS UNION

HUNG is the seed syllable for the union of space and light, emptiness and clarity, heart and mind. Its vibrational energy is related to blue light and to the energy center at our heart.

When we sound HUNG, we enter into the heartfelt presence of love, compassion, peace, and joy.

HUNG is Compassion,
Inseparable and all-embracing,
responsible and ready,
yearning, relieving suffering.

HUNG is Loving and Kind,
Caring and cherishing,
unconditional, radiant, nonjudgmental.

HUNG is Joy,
Unstoppable, uplifting energy,
arising with inspiration and gratitude.

HUNG is Equanimity,
Enlightened unity of heart and mind,
Oneness of balance, harmony, and peace.

Stroke Sequence for Drawing HUNG:

RAM IS FIRE

RAM is the seed syllable for the fire element. Its vibrational energy is associated with red light and the navel chakra.

When we sound RAM, we connect to the strength, vitality, and creativity of our inner fire.

> RAM is Strength,
> Rising up with energy and perseverance.

> RAM is Vitality,
> Able and complete,
> Dancing with universal life and love.

> RAM is Creativity,
> Our spark of joy and upwelling expression.

> RAM is Generating,
> Burning, digesting, ripening,
> source of inner warmth.

Stroke sequence for drawing RAM:

DZA IS PERFECT ACTION

DZA is the seed syllable for perfect action. Its vibrational energy is associated with green light and the secret chakra.

When we sound DZA, we connect to action that flows perfectly, spontaneously, and effortlessly.

DZA is Perfect,
Timeless, beneficial action.

DZA is Spontaneous,
Connected and confident.

DZA is Effortless,
An overflowing cup, a wish-fulfilling gem.

DZA is the Fruit
of the warrior syllables.

Stroke sequence for drawing DZA:

20. The Five Warrior Seed Syllable Practice

> With practice I can go deeper,
> I can understand more clearly,
> I can be more effective,
> I can free myself, spontaneously.
> With practice I can change everything
> from inside to out.

THE FIVE WARRIOR seed syllable practice is used to clear physical, emotional, and psychological disturbances by directing our attention through breath, sound, and visualization.

Sounding the seed syllables while connecting to their energetic qualities is connecting to our own true nature. It is a process of cultivating and opening to the positive qualities that are always there within.

STEP BY STEP: THE FIVE WARRIOR SEED SYLLABLE PRACTICE

1. Sit comfortably in the five-point posture (see page 74).
2. Visualize your body as a sacred luminous body with the five pure lights of the five main chakras and three energy channels (see page 109).
3. Purify your inner energy by doing the nine-breath purification practice (see page 108).
4. Now, visualize and sound each syllable, one after another, starting with AH, as follows:

AH

▸ Visually:	Imagine a white AH at your crown chakra.
▸ Physically:	Breathe in deeply through your nostrils as you put your hands together in the prayer position and touch them to the top of your forehead.
▸ Mentally:	Invoke the qualities of infinite space—vast, pure, open, changeless.
▸ Vocally:	Sound one long AH for as long as comfortably possible before having to take another breath.

OM

▸ Visually:	Imagine a red OM at your throat.
▸ Physically:	Take the next deep breath through your nostrils as you bring your hands, still in prayer mudra, to your throat.
▸ Mentally:	Invoke the qualities of clear light—pure, luminous; awareness, empowered speech.
▸ Vocally:	Sound one long OM for as long as comfortably possible before having to take another breath.

HUNG

▸ Visually:	Imagine a blue HUNG at your heart.
▸ Physically:	Take the next deep breath through your nostrils as you bring your hands, still in prayer mudra, to your heart.
▸ Mentally:	Invoke the qualities of the space/light union—compassion, loving kindness, joy, equanimity
▸ Vocally:	Sound one long HUNG for as long as comfortably possible before having to take another breath.

RAM

- ▸ Visually   Imagine a red RAM at your navel.
- ▸ Physically   Take the next deep breath through your nostrils as you rest your hands on your knees, either palms down with fingers outstretched or palms up with the index fingertip touching the tip of the thumb.
- ▸ Mentally   Invoke qualities of fire: strength, vitality, creativity, generating
- ▸ Vocally   Sound one long RAM for as long as comfortably possible before having to take another breath.

DZA

- ▸ Visually: Imagine a green DZA at your secret chakra.
- ▸ Physically: Take the next deep breath through your nostrils as you rest your hands on your knees, either palms down with fingers outstretched or palms up with the index fingertip touching the tip of the thumb.
- ▸ Mentally: Invoke qualities of perfect action—perfect, spontaneous, effortless, fruit.
- ▸ Vocally: Sound one long DZA for as long as comfortably possible before having to take another breath.

5. This completes one round of practice. Repeat for three or five rounds.

6. End with a special breath of blessing (as described on page 53): Blow your own breath up into your nostrils, directing it there with your lower lip. Inhale and receive that breath as a blessing for yourself. As you exhale, visualize sharing that blessing and any benefit from this practice by blowing it out to all beings everywhere.

PRACTICE VARIATIONS

Following are two variations of the practice. They offer different ways of repeating the syllables and are done without any hand movements.

CHANTING THE SYLLABLE COMBINATION

After finishing the first three steps described above, repeat the combined string of syllables—AH OM HUNG RAM DZA—in the following manner:

- Start slowly, chanting them all in one long breath.
- Gradually speed up the chant until you are saying AH OM HUNG RAM DZA as fast as you can, with many recitations of the combination per breath.
- Gradually slow down the number of recitations per breath, letting your voice fade to a whisper, then drop into silence.
- This completes one round. Do three to five rounds.

CHANTING SINGLE SYLLABLES

In this practice, after finishing the first three steps, one warrior syllable is visualized, as described above, and then sounded several times in a row:

- Take a deep breath and sound one long syllable for the full length of the outbreath.
- Take another breath and sound the same syllable again, in one long sound for the full length of the breath. Repeat for a total of three to five times.
- Then sound each of the other syllables in the same way, three to five times.
- This completes the practice.

THE CHANGE YOU BECOME

As you sound the five warrior seed syllables, imagine that thousands and millions of other beings, including plants and animals, are chanting with you.

> Sing until all you hear are these sounds.
> Sing until all you see are these symbols.
> Sing until you transform into the qualities of the mantra.

Conclusion

THE HEALING POWER of breath lies in the way it can be used to focus and transform the mind. Attending to it will bring balance, meaning, and purpose to your life.

All of the main breathing exercises I have described in this book—from meditation, tonglen, and the nine-breath purification to *tsa lung* and the five warrior seed syllables—have been used for thousands of years with great benefit by thousands of spiritual practitioners. The results of regular practice are clear: less stress; more confidence; a calmer, clearer mind; and a stronger, healthier body.

The wisdom and essence of these teachings are beneficial not only temporarily, in this life, but ultimately, in the liberation of ourselves and all beings from the endless cycles of worldly suffering.

If you are holding this book, you are holding many of the most precious teachings, methods, and insights that have been passed down to me by my spiritual teachers. You are also holding my gratitude for them and for this opportunity to share with you what I have learned.

Every reader has different connections, needs, and challenges. My hope is that some of the many practices described here will become medicine for the healing and transformation of your life, and, through that, for the benefit of those all around you.

Appendix 1: The Tibetan Bön Tradition

The union of compassion and wisdom is the heart of the 84,000 teachings of Tönpa Shenrab. Through their compassion, Tibetan Bön Masters shared their wisdom with the world, and people of the five directions received the benefit like sunflowers welcoming the sun.

YUNGDRUNG BÖN

BÖN IS THE OLDEST of the five main spiritual traditions of Tibet. It has been the indigenous religion of the Himalayas for thousands of years and is the source of Tibetan spiritual culture. The Bön tradition in Tibet is often referred to as Tibetan Bön Buddhism. This is somewhat confusing as the term Buddhism is most commonly understood to describe followers of the great Indian teacher and buddha Shakyamuni Buddha. Bönpos honor Shakyamuni, but their deep lineage connection is to the founder of Bön, Tönpa Shenrab, who predates Shakyamuni by thousands of years.

My tradition is more accurately called Yungdrung Bön. *Yung* means "no birth or no beginning," *drung* means "no death or no end," and Bön refers to the immutable essence of the Dharma that serves to protect all beings. So, Yungdrung Bön is the eternal, indestructible essence of everything.

The ancient, sacred Bön symbol for Yungdrung is a left-turning, four-spoked wheel. Hitler found it so captivating and powerful, he appropriated it for his own Nazi political regime, reversing the direction of the spokes.

The ultimate view of Yungdrung Bön is called Dzogchen, the great perfection. The purpose of Dzogchen training is to recognize and remain in the natural state of the mind, a state that is free of ego-attachment and the causes of suffering.

TÖNPA SHENRAB

Buddha Tönpa Shenrab is the founder of the Yungdrung Bön tradition. Bönpos believe that he first came into the Tibetan region about 18,000 years ago from his homeland in the ancient kingdom of Zhang Zhung.

Through Tönpa Shenrab's teaching, Zhang Zhung had become a land of peace and harmony. That peace was noticeably disturbed when six demons from the Kongpo region of Tibet entered Zhang Zhung and stole six horses. There are many dramatic stories about Tönpa Shenrab's pursuit of the demons and eventual recovery of the horses. However, Buddha Shenrab's main concern when entering Tibet was to liberate it from negative and nonvirtuous influence, starting with the Kongpo region. At that time, the Kongpo people were sacrificing animals to the nature spirits and didn't have the ability to understand Tönpa Shenrab's higher teachings, known as *thapshe sungdrel*, the union of compassion and wisdom, or liberating the mind.

Buddha Shenrab was able to negotiate an understanding between Kongpo worshippers and the nature spirits that from that day forward there would be no more animal sacrifice. Instead, he introduced and blessed the powerful and symbolic use of *tormas*. Tormas are offerings made of barley flour. They are shaped to look like yak, sheep, and goats. It is believed that when they are burned, the spirit receives the same kind of energy that was generated through animal sacrifice. With the blessings of Tönpa Shenrab, this new practice led to harmony and contentment for the practitioners, the animals, and the natural forces or spirits. Ever since then, this kind of offering has been used in the Yungdrung Bön tradition during special rituals such as the smoke offering called *sangchod*.

Tönpa Shenrab imparted what he could during his short stay in Kongpo and left with the deep yearning that someday his first cycle of teachings, called *The Nine Ways of Bön*, would benefit and liberate the people there. With that future in mind, he hid the teachings by burying the texts nearby.

Today, the Kongpo region is a most sacred and powerful place for Bön practitioners because Tönpa Shenrab liberated it from the domination of the demon prince Khyabpa through his teaching and spiritual power. Tibetan Bönpos go there on pilgrimage for purification, healing, and blessings. There are many signs and sacred places where Tönpa Shenrab stayed, where he taught, and where he engaged in power struggles with Khyabpa. In the end, he tamed the demon through compassion, a quality Khyabpa did not have.

TÖNPA SHENRAB'S TEACHINGS

Tönpa Shenrab gave many teachings. His first series or cycle of teachings is called *The Nine Ways of Bön*. The first four ways are known as the Causal Ways. The next five are known as the Result Ways, including the ninth way that contains teachings on Dzogchen.

Causal Bön is concerned with the dynamics of the natural world, including the nature of the five elements and how we interact with them. It also includes rituals and medicines that promote health, healing, and a balanced relationship with the environment and the unseen spiritual forces that are a part of it.

Result Bön is aimed at generating an awakened heart by training the mind. It is concerned with questions of interior development: What are the causes of suffering? How can we be free of them? How can we cultivate compassion for ourselves and others? All of the teachings in Result Bön boil down to the union of compassion and wisdom. It is said that if a teaching does not have this union at heart, it is not Yungdrung Bön.

The second cycle of Tönpa Shenrab's teachings includes the Four Portals and the Fifth Treasure. They are antidotes for the inner five negative emotions: ignorance, attachment, anger, jealousy, and pride.

The third cycle of teachings is called Chi, Nang, Sang: outer, inner, secret, or Sutra, Tantra, Dzogchen. They are antidotes for the three poisons of the mind that create suffering: ignorance, attachment, and anger.

Ultimately, ignorance is the root of all the negative emotions and suffering. The highest teaching from all three cycles is Dzogchen, the Great Perfection. This is the antidote to ignorance.

Today, although some tribes in areas bordering Tibet remain adherents of prehistoric Bön (predating Tönpa Shenrab), all Bönpos in Tibet are Yungdrung Bön practitioners, including those called "New Bön" or "Bön Sarma" who include Drenpa Namkha and Guru Padmasambhava as central refuge figures.

RISE, FALL, AND REVIVAL

Bön was the only religion in Tibet and throughout the kingdom of Zhang Zhung until the seventh century. This golden age came to an end when Buddhism from India was established as the principal religion of Tibet by Songtsen Gampo, the thirty-third king of Tibet. This was further reinforced by Trisong Detsen, the thirty-eighth king, who killed King Ligmincha, the last king of Zhang Zhung. This started a period of persecution that aimed to convert or eradicate Yungdrung Bön practitioners. During this time, many Bön texts were buried or otherwise hidden to keep them from being destroyed.

Very little is known about the plight of Bönpos from the seventh century to the revival of Yungdrung Bön in the eleventh century. That revival began when Shenchen Luga discovered a number of important hidden scriptures. Through his efforts and organization, Bön emerged again as a full spiritual or religious system. By the fourteenth century, there were a number of large monastic centers of Bön study, the most important of which was Yeru Wansaka. This monastery was destroyed by flooding and eventually replaced in 1405 with the founding of Menri Monastery by Nyame Sherab Gyaltsen. Menri, along with Yungdrung Ling and Kharna (established in the nineteenth century), became the main Bön learning centers. By the twentieth century, there were 330 Bönpo monastic study centers in Tibet.

THE GIFT OF BÖN TO THE WORLD

In 1959, the Chinese occupied Tibet, starting another period of persecution and exile, this time for both Bönpos and Buddhists. Not only was there unimaginable loss of human life, but there was also the loss of over six thousand monasteries along with all of the Dharma texts and support items they housed.

Thanks to the bravery, brilliance, and tireless work of Bönpo leaders, especially His Holiness the late Thirty-Third Menri Trizin and His Eminence Yongdzin Tenzin Namdak Rinpoche, Bön is now flourishing outside of Tibet. These two masters, along with many other Bönpo geshes, lamas, and monks, survived the trauma of fleeing over the Himalayas and made it to safety in Nepal and India. Their escape to freedom opened the gates to share the gift of Yungdrung Bön with the world. In 1961, with the support of the Rockefeller Foundation, over seventy high lamas from different traditions were invited to study in England, including His Holiness the Thirty-Third Menri Trizin, His Eminence Yongdzin Rinpoche, and Samten Karmay from the Bön tradition.

Over the next three years, Yongdzin Rinpoche worked there with Tibetologist David Snellgrove to translate and publish *The Nine Ways of Bön*. This was the first Western scholarly study of the Bönpo tradition using original sources.

Meanwhile, many Bönpo refugees made their way into the Himachal Pradesh area of northwestern India, where they were put to work building roads. They suffered terribly from the harsh conditions, many falling ill and dying. With help from the Catholic Relief Service, they were able to secure enough funds to buy some land in Dolanji (near Solan, Himachal Pradesh) for a Bönpo settlement where families were given a parcel of land and a house. The settlement was fully established in 1967. In 1969, His Holiness Lungtok Tenpai Nyima Rinpoche was selected to be the head of the Tibetan Bön tradition as the Thirty-Third Menri Trizin—the abbot of Menri Monastery. He continued to oversee the building of Menri Monastery in exile, starting with the creation of a new monastic community, a library, an abbot's residence, and then the main temple, which was under construction from 1969 to 1978.

A campaign was organized to collect Bönpo texts from the ancient Bön villages of the Dolpo region in Nepal, bordering Tibet. When a sufficient number of these texts had been published, a lama's college was opened, with the first graduates receiving their geshe degrees in 1986.

Yongdzin Rinpoche left India, returning to Kathmandu to establish another Bönpo monastery and college called Triten Norbutse, formally founded in 1987.

Menri Monastery in India and Triten Norbutse Monastery in Kathmandu are the most important education centers for Bön monks outside of Tibet. Due to the tremendous kindness and courage of His Holiness the Thirty-Third Menri Trizin and His Eminence Yongdzin Rinpoche, there are now hundreds of geshe graduates teaching in many different centers around the world, including the spiritual education center of Sherab Chammaling, founded by Geshe YongDong Losar in Canada.

In 2005, Yongdzin Rinpoche established an international Bön teaching center in France, called Shenten Dargye Ling, for the preservation of Bön and its transmission to Western students. More information about Bön and this center can be found at www.shenten.org.

BÖNPO SCRIPTURES

Bönpo scriptures are divided into two categories: the actual words of Tönpa Shenrab, called the Kanjur, and commentaries related to the Kanjur, called the Katen. Together, they are known as the Canon.

The Kanjur consists of 113 volumes that are divided into four sections: *do de, bum de, gyu de,* and *dzo de.*

Do de is a category of sutric teachings, including monastic rules, biographies of Tönpa Shenrab, and prayers to cure people and problems.

Bum de[20] is a category of teachings that includes such topics as the ten paramitas, bodhicitta, and refuge, but is primarily concerned with the concept of emptiness and the perfection of wisdom.

Gyu de is the category of tantric teachings.

Dzo de is Dzogchen teachings and practices. If a student is ready, Dzogchen is considered to be the highest teaching.

The Katen consists of 293 volumes, including commentaries on the Kanjur and texts on rituals, art, logic, medicine, astrology, and poetry.

Ultimately, the purpose of all of these teachings is to liberate us from suffering and bring peace and happiness to all living beings through the union of compassion and wisdom.

BÖNPO DEITIES

Bönpo deities are projections used in tantric practice to visualize and internalize specific virtuous qualities. They are classified into four categories of the manifestation of compassion: peaceful, semi-peaceful,[21] wrathful, and extremely wrathful. Following are a few examples:

- ▸ the peaceful wisdom-loving mother, Sherab Chamma;
- ▸ the peaceful god of compassion, Shenlha Ödkar;
- ▸ the semi-peaceful Nampar Gyalwa;
- ▸ the semi-peaceful Sangchok Gyalpo and Kyema Ödtso;
- ▸ the wrathful Yeshe Walmo;
- ▸ and the extremely wrathful Sidpai Gyalmo.

Different rituals and practices have their own divinities and methods of visualizing and identifying with them.

There are also deities known as the Protectors of Bön who are guardians of both its doctrines and its practitioners. The most important of these is Sidpai Gyalmo, the Queen of Existence, who is the most wrathful manifestation of Sherab Chamma, the wisdom-loving mother of all buddhas.

Appendix 2: Bön Cosmology

Countless atoms are gathered,
like dust, from all directions,
eventually becoming form.

THERE ARE MANY different levels of Bön teachings, related to the different levels of learning capacity held by individual living beings. The validity of each level has to do with the individual's potential for reception and understanding. The levels are not viewed comparatively as inherently better or worse, greater or lesser.

Each level of capacity has different perceptions regarding the existence of the universe. Therefore, in the Bön tradition, there is not necessarily just one creator that created everything. There are three different ways of explaining the origin of the universe according to the three main traditional views or philosophical systems, known as Sutra, Tantra, and Dzogchen.

BÖN SUTRIC COSMOLOGY

In the sutric philosophical system, the existence of the universe is based on atoms. Countless atoms are gathered like dust from all directions, eventually becoming form.

Within this system, there are two types of universe: outer and inner. The outer universe is sometimes called the outer container. It is comprised of the five elements.

Basically, the inner universe is the contents held by the container.

This refers, most significantly, to living beings. There are six categories, or realms, of beings, each of which is characterized by its own
unique form of suffering: worldly god (seemingly perfect conditions
that eventually collapse in a sudden, revolting way), demi-god (constant turmoil of conflict and warring with the gods), human (marked
by jealously and competition with one another), animal (oppression
and abuse stemming from an inability to communicate with language), hungry ghost (beings with very thin necks and huge stomachs
representing endless hunger, thirst, and overwhelming desire that can
never be satisfied), and hell (marked by the unimaginable suffering
of perpetually burning or freezing).

The elements are interdependent and arise in order, one out of the
other. Space is built on emptiness. It exists due to the karmic conditions of the universe and living beings. Wind evolves out of space and
is dependent on it. Fire exists due to the movement of wind. Water
exists because of fire, and earth exists because of water. They emerge
out of each other and stand, dependent upon each other, like a stack
of blocks.

Starting with the space element, the outer container evolves from
the bottom up. The process is like constructing a building, where one
floor provides the foundation for the next.

Living beings of the inner universe, on the other hand, evolve from
the top down. The process is like descending stairs, starting with the
god realm, then demi-god, human, animal, hungry ghost, and finally,
the hell realm.

The Bön sutric cosmological story starts with the existence of the
container, including the earth. A being of light from the god realm,
known as Ödsal Lha, came to earth because of a previous experience
there. Ödsal Lha's body was an entity beyond solid form, like light
itself; *ödsal* means light and *lha* means god. The sun and moon were
not visible due to the intensity of Ödsal Lha's light. It shone all around
him, thousands of miles in all directions.

During this primordial time, the oceans and lakes of the earth were
very nutritious and delicious. Ödsal Lha ended up drinking the water.

As he touched and drank from the ocean, he became held by gravity, unable to fly back to where he came from. After drinking, he grew hungry, as well. He became more dependent on the earth and the five elements, and as he partook of solid plant food, his light diminished and he became more solid and heavy. Then he wished and prayed that other beings of light, like himself, would come and join him. His desire became a karmic condition and they did as he wished.

As their god qualities faded, the demi-god realm emerged. Time passed and eventually, through disagreements and territorial divisions, the demi-god realm degraded into the human realm, marked by jealousy and competition. The human realm degraded into the three lower realms of animal, hungry ghost, and hell. That devolution is portrayed in the following story:

There were three men living on earth who created the three lower realms through their emotional response to circumstance. Man A had some fruit. Man B stole the fruit. Man C witnessed the theft.

Man A was a victim who became very upset and angry due to his loss. He didn't know who stole his fruit, so he became very suspicious of everyone. He embodied anger and entered the hell realm. Man B was a thief who gave into his desire. He embodied greed and entered the hungry ghost realm. Man C was a witness who had no idea if he should keep the whole thing a secret or if he should tell A or tell B. He embodied confusion and ignorance and entered the animal realm.

This is how the three realms came into existence through the power of the three poisons of emotion. The story serves as a warning about how our choices and emotional responses can lock us into degraded states of being. In this story, the victim actually creates more negative energy than the criminal by generating the intense and extremely damaging emotions of anger and suspicion.

I had a friend who lived this story when his bike was stolen. He had no idea who would do such a thing and began to suspect many people. He also became noticeably upset, angry, and agitated. I told him the story of the three lower realms and reminded him that he really didn't know who stole the bike and should be careful not to let negative emotions escalate through anger and suspicion. The theft is one piece of bad karma, but suspecting ten people is like creating ten pieces of bad karma. Without care and awareness, the negative emotional involvement of the victim can outstrip that of the criminal. In this case, my friend told me that when he finally let go of his anger and his bike, he got his bike back through others who found and returned it to him.

BÖN TANTRIC COSMOLOGY

According to the Bön tantric system, Trigyal Khugpa is a god representing the unification of space. He created the universe by blowing his breath out into the emptiness of space. This gave birth to the space and wind elements. Then, the movement of his magic tongue caused lightning and the creation of the fire element. The movement of both his breath and tongue caused spit and the birth of the water element. The combined activity of wind, fire, and water created dust and the earth element.

So, in the tantric view, the universe came into being through the breath of Trigyal Khugpa. It came alive by the power of his breath and the "magic tongue of movement." This is known as the general or universal breath. As mentioned earlier, the individual breath is drawn from and dissolves back into the universal breath.

DZOGCHEN COSMOLOGY

In the Dzogchen system, the universe is built out of the clear light of two eggs. One is dark (or black) and is called *Mun kal*, the eon of the dark egg. It is characterized by the absence of enlightened beings and therefore of their guidance. One is light (or white) and is called *Dron kal*, the eon of the white egg. It is characterized by the possibility of beings becoming enlightened and of guidance from enlightened beings, or buddhas.

The notion of the egg alludes to the energy of the universe taking shape, or form, out of the formless. Both eggs are clear light and primordial aspects of the universe. All existence has its origin in this clear light, whether it is black or white.

From clear light, the five pure lights emerge as primordial sources. For example, the solid earth element comes from beyond solid earth, arising from pure yellow light. The solid water element comes from beyond solid water, arising from pure blue light. Likewise, fire arises from pure red light, wind from pure green light, and space from pure white light.

Ultimately then, in the Dzogchen view, the universe comes from white and black light. As with Dzogchen itself, the emergence of the universe rests in the nonconceptual and is beyond ideas and explanations. The universe, and everything in it, also has the two aspects of Dzogchen: primordial purity and spontaneous arising. The primordial, or ultimate, aspect is pure awareness that is primordially perfected and beyond conception. The spontaneous, or relative, view is the primordial, spontaneous arising of energy and form. As in the Dzogchen basic view of universal existence, everything comes out of pure emptiness, remains in it, and merges back into emptiness.

Notes

1. *Tönpa* is the Tibetan word for buddha.
2. For more information about Tibetan Yungdrung Bon, see appendix 1.
3. *La* refers to the deepest level of our existence. It is understood to be a fine balance of the five primordial elemental energies. These energies come together in relation to the vast net of cause and effect that gives rise to our unique character and capacity as a human being. In Tibet, *la* is understood as part of the triad *la, yi,* and *sem* (soul, consciousness, and mind). It is also understood as one of five basic energies: *tsok, lu, wang tang, lung ta,* and *la* (life force, health, prosperity, reputation or rapport, and soul or mental confidence). These shared notions are part of Tibetan culture and underpin common practices related to, for example, Tibetan astrology and rituals such as the life force and soul retrieval ceremonies.
4. Trigyal Khugpa is a god figure representing the unification of space. Unlike the Western understanding of god, both Trigyal Khugpa as creator and his creation are understood to be impermanent.
5. There are eight modes of consciousness including the consciousness of each of the five senses (eyes, ears, nose, mouth, body) and the mind. The seventh one is an afflictive consciousness that carries emotions and karmic traces. The eighth consciousness is the *künzhi namshe,* the base consciousness out of which all the others arise.
6. Tibetan medicine views the gall bladder as one of three main roots of disease.
7. See chapter 16 for a full description of the *tsa lung trul khor* exercises.
8. The three doors are body, speech, mind. The three realms are desire, form, and formless. The three times are past, present, future. The three bodies are the three spiritual dimensions known as the *dharmakaya, sambhogakaya,* and *nirmanakaya.*
9. These include dopamine, serotonin, oxytocin, and endorphins.
10. These chemicals include endorphins, growth hormone, melatonin, DHEA (dehydroepiandrosterone), GABA (gamma aminobutyric acid), and melatonin.
11. Bönpos consider the ring finger to have a connection to the heart and to the spirit. The thumb is often placed on the ring finger (or thumbs on the ring

fingers) to highlight this association before using the ring finger to, for example, touch oneself or another in blessing, dip in water that is then flicked out in offering, or in this case, close a nostril in a sacred breathing exercise.

12. Green is the color associated with the air element.

13. Dark smoke is gone from the white and red channels. All that is left is the red and white that mixes as pink now in the central channel and is expelled.

14. To view a video demonstration of the five *tsa lung* exercises go to www.sherabchammaling.com/teachings/videos.

15. The Tibetan word *bardo* literally means "intermediate state" or "in-between state." There are many kinds of *bardo*, but the word is most often used to refer to the state between death and rebirth.

16. To view this video of the Sherab Chamma Heart Mantra go to www.sherabchammaling.com/teachings/videos.

17. *Sadhana* is the Sanskrit work for *choka*.

18. Sherab Chamma's seed syllable is HRI. It is pronounced by curling up the sides of the tongue and pressing them against the back teeth while saying what sounds like *shree* as heard in the word *shriek* but blended with a lot of air from the back of the throat, as in the word *he*.

19. All forty letters of the Tibetan alphabet are considered sacred.

20. *Bum* literally means "one hundred thousand," referring to the number of mantras required to complete one cycle for each of the nine traditional preliminary practices called *ngöndro*. These are daily spiritual practices that ground the practitioner in a living connection with the lama, Buddha, Dharma, and sangha while cultivating the qualities of wisdom and compassion that lead to enlightenment for the benefit of oneself and all living beings. The different ngöndro practices or methods include visualization, meditation, purification, receiving empowerment, making offerings, and mantra recitation.

21. The Tibetan term translated as "semi-peaceful" literally means "increasing" and refers to a manifestation with both peaceful qualities and escalating or ever-increasing wrathful energy.

About the Author

GESHE YONGDONG LOSAR (Geshela) is a Tibetan Bön lama, or spiritual teacher, in the Yungdrung Bön lineage, which is rooted in the indigenous spiritual tradition of the Himalayas. He lives in Courtenay, British Columbia, where he established and directs Sherab Chamma Ling, the only Tibetan Bön Buddhist Center in Canada. He teaches in many centers and universities around the world and has also founded the Bon Da Ling center in Costa Rica.

Geshela has published several books in Tibetan and is an active member of Chiling Bön Tsok, the International Bön Lamas Association, and the International Tibetan Non-Sectarian Religious Association. He is cherished by students and colleagues for his calm and loving manner, his humor and humility, and his tireless dedication to the Dharma and the ultimate liberation of hearts and minds.

Geshe YongDong was born in 1969 in the Ngawa County of Amdo in northeastern Tibet. As a boy, his desire to become a monk was intensified by the death of his mother, the death of his grandmother, and the three years he spent alone in the harsh Himalayan mountains tending a flock of over six hundred sheep for his uncle. At the age of thirteen his uncle finally allowed Geshela to enter the Nangzhig Monastery in Amdo, the largest Bön monastery in Tibet, where he studied under the venerable masters Geshe Wako Gyaltsen, Yongdzin Yeshe Gyaltsen, Jawob Rinpoche, and Jetsun Namkha Tsultrim.

Eleven years later, after completing specialized training in all aspects of the Dharma, he was awarded the *geshe* degree, an academic achievement of the highest order, similar to a Western PhD in theology. He escaped Tibet soon after, settling in India where he had the honor of receiving teachings from some of the most eminent spiritual leaders of our time: His Holiness the Dalai Lama; His Holiness the Thirty-Third Menri Trizin, the spiritual leader of Bön; and His Eminence Yongdzin Tenzin Namdak Rinpoche, the senior teacher and lineage holder of Bön; and Venerable Ponlop Trinley Nyima Rinpoche, the main teacher at Menri Monastery.

Geshela spent another three years studying at Sera Monastic University in southern India under Venerable Geshe Thupten Rinchen before relocating to Canada.

ABOUT THE EDITOR

Bernadette Wyton met Geshe YongDong in 2002 while he was teaching a course on meditation at the college in her hometown of Port Alberni, British Columbia. She has been his student ever since and has served as his writing assistant for the last ten years.

She has received teachings from other precious Bön lamas including His Eminence Yongdzin Tenzin Namdak Rinpoche and Khenpo Tenpa Yungdrung Rinpoche and remains a grateful witness to the clarity of their wisdom, the excellence of their teachings, and the blessing that flows through them for the benefit of all.

Bernadette lives with her husband on Vancouver Island, where they enjoy the ocean, growing their own food, and being with their children and grandchildren.

What to Read Next
from Wisdom Publications

Tibetan Yoga
Magical Movements of Body, Breath, and Mind
Alejandro Chaoul

Discover ancient Tibetan yogic practices that integrate body, breath, and mind on the journey to personal cultivation and enlightenment.

Mindfulness Yoga
The Awakened Union of Breath, Body, and Mind
Frank Jude Boccio

Editor's Choice—*Yoga Journal*

The Six Lamps
Secret Dzogchen Instructions of the Bön Tradition
Jean-Luc Achard

"*The Six Lamps* guides us into the world of Dzogchen. . . . A major contribution to the study and practice of Dzogchen, this book offers a glimpse of Bön's highest teachings."—*Buddhadharma*

About Wisdom Publications

Wisdom Publications is the leading publisher of classic and contemporary Buddhist books and practical works on mindfulness. To learn more about us or to explore our other books, please visit our website at wisdomexperience.org or contact us at the address below.

Wisdom Publications
199 Elm Street
Somerville, MA 02144 USA

We are a 501(c)(3) organization, and donations in support of our mission are tax deductible.

Wisdom Publications is affiliated with the Foundation for the Preservation of the Mahayana Tradition (FPMT).